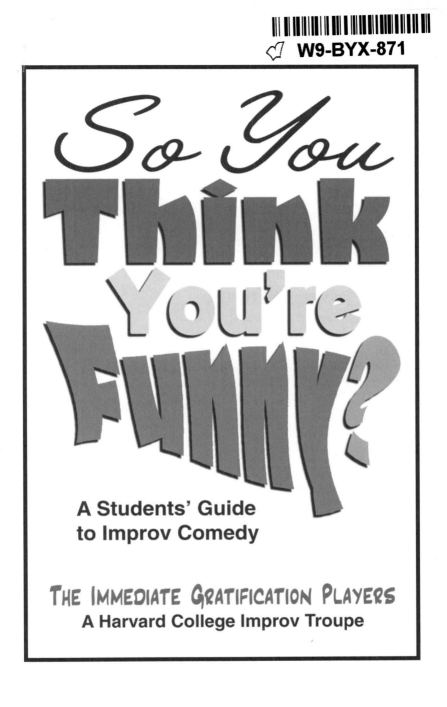

So You Think You're Funny?

A Students' Guide
to Improv Comedy

THE IMMEDIATE GRATIFICATION PLAYERS
A Harvard College Improv Troupe

MERIWETHER PUBLISHING LTD.
Colorado Springs, Colorado

Meriwether Publishing Ltd., Publisher
PO Box 7710
Colorado Springs, CO 80933-7710

www.meriwether.com

Executive Editor: Theodore O. Zapel
Assistant Editor: Amy Hammelev
Cover design: Jan Melvin

Copyright © 2010 Meriwether Publishing Ltd.
Printed in the United States of America
First edition

Library of Congress Cataloging-in-Publication Data

So you think you're funny? : a students' guide to improv comedy / by The Immediate Gratification Players. -- 1st ed.
    p. cm.
  ISBN 978-1-56608-173-3
  1. Improvisation (Acting) 2. Stand-up comedy. I. Immediate Gratification Players (Comedy troupe)
  PN2071.I5S575 2010
  792'.028--dc22

                                 2010033418

1   2   3   10   11   12

To the holy fish
and the rest of the extended IGP family

TABLE OF CONTENTS

Foreword

If you are holding this book in your hand, having purchased it, or are considering purchasing it, I guess you are interested in improv. I heartily endorse that interest. Long ago, in the waning days of the twentieth century, I didn't do improv either. And then I did. And I haven't stopped since.

As a college freshman, I joined the Immediate Gratification Players (IGP) because I saw a show and they made me laugh. I thought improv comedy looked fun and would be a frivolous addition to the otherwise extremely serious extracurriculars I had planned for myself.

I underestimated improv, or, as it is called by people who like extra syllables, "improvisation." IGP changed my life. The nervous college freshman who wanted to be a senator is now a neurotic thirty-something comedy writer. Although some would say that this choice was "unconventional" or "stupid," I think I made the right decision. The Senate is a partisan disaster and I can wear flip-flops to work.

Of course, you don't have to throw your *whole* professional life away for improv. There are lots of résumé-bolstering reasons to consider learning improvisation. In fact, business schools all over the country offer improv workshops because they believe it will improve your listening skills, make you more open-minded, a better collaborator, and a more confident person in "public speaking" scenarios.

These are all true. If you are a devoted student of improv, you will hone your listening, cooperating, and speaking skills. You will also become 64 percent more sexually attractive.[1] But the most important reason to do improv is that it is play. That's right. Play — the verb, the thing you do, not the thing by Shakespeare you go see in a theatre. And play is something that adults don't get to do very often. Our culture tells us that playing means spending money on resort vacations, or fancy luxury items, or theme restaurants, or casinos. That can be *fun,* but it doesn't make it *play* just because your drink is blue and has an umbrella in it.

---

1. To other improvisers. Sorry.

1

I can go into a lot of the reasons, that even health professionals say playing is important for adults, but I was not paid for this so I am not going to do any research. Off the top of my head I've made up a few reasons already: play makes you interesting, play keeps you from turning into your parents, play makes children love you, and play gives you immunity in the next super-plague.

Improvisation is real play. It is about using yourself and not judging yourself. It is about playing with your friends to create hilarity. It is about being imaginative in a way you haven't been since you played as a kid. It is about laughing. It is about learning to relax again and have fun and trust that the people onstage with you will take care of you.

So what are you waiting for? Say yes.

— Sarah Haskins
Professional Comedy Type

Chapter Zero
So You Think You're Funny? An Introduction

Hello and welcome! We are the Immediate Gratification Players, Harvard University's premier (and only!) long-form improvisational comedy troupe. For the next hour, we are going to shower you with unscripted hilarity! But before we start our show, can we get from the audience a one-word suggestion on which we will base our comedy? OK, someone said the word book. So without further ado, IGP presents: a book!

We are the Immediate Gratification Players, and we have been doing improvisational comedy for over two decades. In this book, we want to show you how to do it, too.

We call this book a "students' guide" to improv. We want to define student broadly, from elementary school on through college — and beyond. Students of any age can pick up this book, read it through, put it down, and start performing hilarious improv. Maybe it will be rough at first, but we truly believe anyone can be a very funny improviser.

Over the course of this book, you will read lots about IGP (as we call it) — our history and the stories we have to tell. For over a decade, we have hosted our Laugh Riot Festival, bringing in improv troupes from all over the country. We have also performed across the nation — Los Angeles, New York, Chicago — and even internationally in Canada and England.

But enough about us. Let's not let this conversation be one-sided. What about you? What's your deal?

OK, well maybe by the end of this book you'll warm up to us.

This book is divided into two parts. The first half, called Building the Skills, will focus on honing the craft. It has useful drills, important rules to remember, and a basic tutorial in building your very first improv scene. It discusses various forms of improv to allow you to decide *what kind* of improv you want to do.

The second half, called Storming the Stage, will show you how to put your product in front of an audience. From creating a troupe, to publicizing a performance, to treating your audience right, this is the book that will make you *show-worthy*.

So read onward. We bet you'll be funnier in no time. Or in some time. Or in a lot of time, if you are a slow reader.

On with the show!

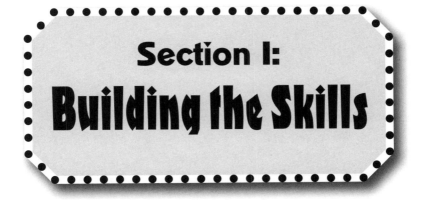

Section I:
Building the Skills

"NICE TO MEET YOU — I'M THE STRAIGHT MAN."

Chapter One
IMPROVISATIONAL COMEDY: TELL ME MORE

Improvisational comedy. Who? What? When? Where? Why? How? These are the questions typically answered by journalists and birthday invitations, but they are also a great place to start our foray into the wonders of improv.

Maybe you saw improv for the first time fifty years ago or maybe you have never seen it before in your life. Either way, consider this chapter an introduction to improv and a chance to get acquainted.

But before you dive in, remember what improv really is: an addictive, ridiculous funfest. You can save the damsel (or dude-sel) in distress, get eaten by lions, and blast off to the moon, all in five minutes onstage ...

Think of your favorite play, your favorite work of theatre. See it performed onstage and picture the actors going through their paces.

OK, now take all the props off this imaginary stage. Throw away the set. There is no furniture, nothing to hold on to. Now strip the actors naked, and avert your eyes if you are inclined. Put them in street clothing, and take away their scripts. The actors must make up everything, and every single performance of this play becomes completely unique.

Such is improv. No lines, no plans: each performance is distinct. It can be dramatic or, more popularly, it can be *comedic*. This book will discuss the latter — improvisation that comes with the added challenge of humor.

You can see it on the stage, on television, in cities across the nation and all over the globe. There are professionals onstage, students in classes, and people of all ages in troupes. It seems like everyone is doing improv these days.

Sure, it is still not as popular a hobby as the guitar, but when did a guitar ever make you laugh? The next time you try to impress your date with a melodious strummed serenade, instead think improv comedy!

The Brief (or, Sort of Brief) History of Improv

For as long as people have wanted to perform without having to go to the trouble of writing a script, improv has existed. Historians (and now, IGP) cite a number of early predecessors of modern improv, most notably the Commedia dell'Arte theatre troupes of renaissance Italy, which used basic scenarios and sketches to structure their otherwise unscripted shows. However, improv mostly remained the stuff of rehearsals and theatre classes until the middle of the twentieth century.

While improv may have been helpful in sharpening an actor's skills, scripts were still considered a fundamental, inextricable part of what theatre was all about. This sentiment was taken to such extremes that there were actually laws on the books in Great Britain until 1968 that required all scripts be approved by the censors in the Lord Chamberlain's Office, meaning any directors risked criminal prosecution if they allowed their actors to improvise.

Drama teacher Viola Spolin was probably the most important architect of modern improv comedy. As a part of President Franklin D. Roosevelt's New Deal programs, she was charged with introducing theatre to Chicago's poor and unemployed. In search of more straightforward ways to teach the basics of performance to her diverse group of students, she devised a series of games that broke down acting to its component parts and placed a high premium on creativity. These activities proved massively successful, and they formed the basis for the "Theater Games" system, the first major improv comedy tradition.

After a brief sojourn to Hollywood where she used her "Theater Games" to train young actors, Spolin returned to her native Chicago in 1955. By this time, her son Paul Sills had become the director of the fledgling Compass Theater, where he used his mother's techniques to put on unscripted shows based on outlines devised by the actors. A turning point came when the bartender at their venue asked them to keep performing so that he could sell more drinks.

With no more previously devised material available, but eager to please their patron, the Compass Players decided to just wing it and take suggestions from the audience. And so, more or less, modern improv comedy was born at that moment in a Chicago bar, and we have the wondrous mix of alcohol and greed to thank for it. Not that we would ever endorse such vices, but, hey, you cannot argue with results.

The famed Second City Company spun out of the Compass Players in 1959, and the mother-and-son team of Spolin and Sills spent the next decade refining and codifying their ideas on improv. "Theater Games" had now grown into well over 200 exercises, and Spolin published her classic improv text *Improvisation for the Theater* in 1963. Other Compass Players, including Elaine May, *The Graduate* director Mike Nichols, Del Close, and Ted Flicker, also set to work on their own theories of improv.

Along with Viola Spolin's teaching assistant and eventual successor, Jo Forsberg, this group comprised the intellectual founders of modern improv. Beyond dominating the Chicago comedy scene, which was quickly becoming very improv-focused, their ideas achieved national prominence as their pupils, such as John Belushi and Bill Murray, became some of *Saturday Night Live's* first players. Second City remains to this day one of the most important sources of rising comedy stars.

Elsewhere, English drama instructor Keith Johnstone was hard at work demolishing everything thought to be true about theatre. While working as a teacher at London's Royal Court Theatre in the late 1950s, he ordered his students to stop trying to concentrate or be clever. Instead, he demanded they just do whatever was the most obvious thing that popped into their heads.

These counter-intuitive methods — which were, of course, actually meant to be completely *intuitive* — produced more creative and spontaneous actors. Upon moving to Canada in the 1960s, he turned his teaching philosophies into the performance format Theatresports, which pitted opposing teams of improvisers against each other in a contest to see who was funniest. This basic premise influenced the long-running television show *Whose Line Is It Anyway?,* which remains unquestionably the most famous and successful showcase of improv comedy to date.

A Briefer, Faker History of Improv

Although the history you are reading might be true according to "experts" and "books," did you know that improv actually has a far more secret history that stretches back millennia? Well, it totally does!

Improv was first invented some thirty thousand years ago. A pair of enterprising young caveman decided to entertain their fellow Cro-Magnons by humorously reenacting such hilarious scenarios as being eaten by a tiger or going to war with a rival tribe.

When these ideas started to become stale, they created language so that they could better articulate the amusing disparities between how things were ideally supposed to work and how so often reality jarred with these expectations. ("What's the deal with hunting?" proved one of their most popular recurring bits.)

As these ancient shows grew longer and stretched into the night, audiences needed light and warmth to continue enjoying the shows, which forced the cave scientists to finally get their act together and invent fire.

The tribe saw the happiness that these Stone Age improvisers created and so sent them to other caves to spread the joy. Wanting to keep the improvisers fresh for the night's performance, the cavemen invented the wheel so that they could be brought more quickly to their shows.

We do not want to bore you with how agriculture was really invented, but let's just say it involves a little corn and a lot of improv.

IGP PRESENTS:
Improv in the 14th Century

Improv was very different back in the medieval age, but then again, so was comedy as a whole. Philosophers believed that there were four kinds of humor and that comedy resulted from either having too much or too little of each.

There was phlegmatic comedy, which was all about making piercing observations about the world. Choleric comedy was the ancestor of the rant comedy that is so popular today. Sanguine comedy was the most idealistic type of comedy and very popular with medieval twentysomethings (who, due to their much shorter lifespan, were usually around ten or twelve). Melancholic comedy was not exactly funny, but was a pretty reasonable reaction to living in the Middle Ages.

Most improv shows back then involved careful bleeding of the audience so as to achieve the funniest balance of humors. Leeches and plague were also commonly bestowed upon audience members for increased hilarity.

Improv Geography: Not as Complicated as Real Geography

Like any nation, improv has its capital cities and its lesser towns, its villages, and its metropolises. (Improv has no Yellowstone. Yet.)

The biggest improv capital of the world is Chicago. It is the home of Second City, Viola Spolin, and the original cast of *SNL*. But as the importance of improv comedy has increased in the entertainment world, vibrant improv communities have developed in New York and Los Angeles, with troupes like The Upright Citizens Brigade and The Groundlings producing celebrities for the big screen.

Improv is also an *international phenomenon,* with many famous improv comedians coming out of Toronto. In Europe, improv loses its "v," becoming "impro." (Something to do with the time zones ...)

But improv also exists on smaller stages, in cities like San Jose, California, Richmond, Virginia, and Acadia, Maine. The first spacewalk? Entirely improv comedy.

At the college level, most large universities have an improv troupe. At Harvard, we have two. At Yale University, there are four, which means that their games of Chinese Checkers are always much more fun.

And at the high school level, improv flourishes in clubs, troupes, and drama programs. Many high school troupes are affiliated with high school leagues run by local professional theatres, allowing even theatre kids to say, "I made varsity!"

IGP PRESENTS:
Improv Brands

Just like hamburgers have McDonald's and Burger King, improv has its own set of brands. A quick glossary:

The Second City: *A seminal troupe that began in 1959 in Chicago, Second City has trained countless celebrities. It also produced the cult hit television show* SCTV.

The Groundlings: *Founded in 1974 in Los Angeles, The Groundlings also have their share of alumni who have made it big, including Will Ferrell and Conan O'Brien.*

Theatresports: *Created by Keith Johnstone in 1977, Theatresports adds competition to improv and is licensed to theatres.*

ComedySportz: *An offshoot of Theatresports founded in 1984, ComedySportz is located in over twenty cities.*

The Upright Citizens Brigade: *Founded in 1990 by, among others, SNL's Amy Poehler, The UCB is New York City's most celebrated improv theatre.*

ImprovOlympic: *Founded in Chicago in 1981 by Del Close, iO uses a Harold, which has structured group scenes, as its signature format.*

The Immediate Gratification Players: *IGP is a Harvard University improv troupe that wrote a book once.*

The Residents of Improville: The White Pages

Can improv make you rich and famous? While the odds may be slim, Tina Fey and countless other *SNL* alum would likely nod their heads. So would the star correspondents of *The Daily Show,* as well as other television comedies. More and more comedic actors have a background in improv comedy.

But improv is not only the playground of those who have their faces on a billboard. When you see a funny sketch video on YouTube, its conception may have been influenced by improv. Even corporations have their workers learn improvisational techniques to be able to better combat problems they may have in the workplace. (While the corporate value of asking Sharon from sales to cluck like a chicken for twenty minutes as part of a team building exercise may be questionable, we fully support it.)

Countless students perform in troupes at their school or college, from Harvard University to UC Santa Cruz. Some schools have so many students who want to perform they hold auditions. When students are rejected they start their own troupes (as we think they should!).

You need not be in college to be a great improviser. A few years ago, IGP led a workshop for a girl's eighth birthday party. Now there is someone who is getting ahead of the game!

In short, improv is like text messaging or aging — almost everyone seems to be doing it these days.

But Why Improv? Why?

Improv is sort of the opposite of war in that improv is good for absolutely everything except weapon sales. It *bolsters creativity,* it makes people collaborate with their scene partners, it takes people out of their usual comfort zone and makes them take risks, and it does not cost anything to do. Above all, it is incredibly *fun* and *exciting.*

Those are all reasons why improv is such a popular team building exercise in the corporate world. Many professional troupes supplement their earnings from shows by holding learning sessions for businesses. Although the skills Viola Spolin originally zeroed in on were meant to be the component parts of theatre, they have just as much to do with life in general. It turns out being able to work with others, communicate clearly, and deal gracefully with unexpected situations is actually useful.

But that is just what improv can do for the improviser. The reason why most people want to get into improv — and the reason, we would wager, why you are holding this book right now — is because it is an amazing way to *entertain people.*

People want to laugh, and there are few things that are as funny as successful improv shows. So, basically, improv is something that can make you a better, more complete person while making everyone around you extremely happy. What more could you ask for?

IGP PRESENTS:
Better Reasons To Do Improv

Still not sure that improv is a worthwhile activity? Are you going to need some outlandish, completely crazy promises to be convinced that improv is important? Well, OK! Improv is a great way to:

- *Increase your electability! Ever notice how you never win elections for things? Do improv and that is sure to change. Just ask William Howard Taft!*
- *Play chess better! Little known fact: Gary Kasparov was the greatest improviser of the twentieth century. This is not a coincidence.*
- *Win awards! Do you know why Elinor Ostrom and Oliver Williamson won the 2009 Nobel Prize for Economics? All we will say is that it was either their analysis of economic governance or their improv. We have said too much already.*

But How Can I Actually Do This Crazy Improv Thing?

So we covered the *classic* five Ws of improv — what, when, where, who, and why. (We just made up the fact that it was classic.) But still, that leaves the pesky H. How, exactly, do you do improv?

At this point, we have to be honest. There is just no way to answer that question in a few paragraphs, and it would be unfair of us to even try. Honestly, we would need an entire book to answer that question properly. Oh well. Sorry.

Wait, what's that?

Ladies and gentlemen, boys and girls, it has been brought to our attention that IGP does in fact have an entire book at its disposal! This very book, actually. Since we really should not let an opportunity like this go to waste, we probably should go ahead and teach you everything you need to know about how to do improv.

TYPICAL IMPROV SCENE

Chapter Two
A SCENE: THE BASIC UNIT OF IMPROV

All improvisers have a favorite scene — usually the time they thought of a joke that leveled the audience flat. Hearing the story of a favorite scene can often sound like a travelogue: "We were on a ship," "We were getting out of a cop car," "We had just been in the jungle."

Such is the power of improv. A scene can take place anywhere, include any character, and be about anything. Building a great scene is the first step toward creating great improv ...

To master the art of an improv show is to first master the scene. No matter what sort of improv you are doing, everything you do in an improv show will be some sort of *scene,* an interaction between two or more people. If an improv show is a sentence, a scene is one word. And when babies learn to talk, they start with words.

Consistently building good scenes with your fellow performers is the key to successful improv shows, and there are some basic common threads that unite all good improv scenes. Thus, taking you through a great scene is the perfect place to start your improv journey. In this chapter, we will take you step-by-step through a scene to explore the many ways — both good and bad — in which a scene can develop, and we will also introduce a few key bits of terminology that will help make you fluent in the language of improv.

To keep it simple, the scene in this chapter will be one in which the performers enter whenever they choose and there are no restrictions placed upon what they can say and do. In other words, no gimmicks. And in order to focus on that all-important scene, you need to start with *a line.*

What's My Line? Accepting an Offer

Suppose you have read through this whole book, and now you are performing a show. The current scene comes to an end and you step forward to start a new one. Another member of your troupe steps forward at just about the same moment, thus automatically making the two of you scene partners. One of you will have to speak first, allowing that new scene to begin. So where does that first line come from?

If you are doing it right, that line should come out of thin air roughly a millisecond before you actually say it. The idea that improv should *always be spontaneous* is not just a nice sentiment; it is something you want to try your absolute hardest to realize in every scene you do. Sure, it can be easy to come up with lines, characters, and even fairly fleshed out ideas for scenes while you are standing on the sidelines. In fact, it might make you more comfortable to plan your entire scene out in your head in advance.

But part of your job as an improviser is to be able to instantly jettison all those ideas the second you step onstage. Besides the fact that an audience will sniff it out when a line has been planned ahead of time, there is a more obvious reason why you should just trust yourself to come up with something on the spot: *your scene partner might speak first.* If that happens, which it should happen about fifty percent of the time, then it does not matter what you came up with ahead of time, as your sole responsibility is to *accept* whatever your scene partner offered you.

Here is a little secret: this paragraph (the one you are reading right now!) is the most important one in the entire book. If you can take only one thing away, make sure it is this: the most fundamental aspect of good improv is *acceptance*. When your scene partner says a line, chooses an emotion, or uses a physicality to create a sense of your surrounding environment — in short, when he or she *offers* you a piece of information about the scene — you should always, always, always accept this "offer" as true. (Let's hope your partner never says anything extremely offensive ...)

On their most basic level, all improv scenes are really just a steady progression of offers, acceptances, and return offers; it is this pattern that sustains the momentum of any given scene. Whatever the first thing your scene partner says is *true.* You accept it and use that initial offer to inform your next line. Then your partner accepts that offer and says something back to you, which you roll with and respond to. And so on and so forth.

It is also worth keeping in mind that offers do not necessarily have to be verbal. If the first thing your scene partner does is mime taking a can of soda out of a refrigerator, make sure you do not walk through that fridge later in the scene. Because if you deny the reality that your scene partner has created, then you are *blocking* him or her. (See Chapter Three for more on a *"block."*) Sure, it can be something as relatively minor as accidentally walking through a piece of furniture your partner placed in the scene (and in our experience it is just as likely that the person who put the furniture there will forget where it is supposed to be), or it can be something as scene-haltingly awful as saying, "No, you're wrong. That's not true."

It does not matter if you think your scene partner's offer was weak and you can come up with a better one. Once an offer is made, it cannot be taken back, and part of the trust between scene partners is the understanding that each improviser will accept the other's offer. That is not to say that every offer is amazing. Part of the process of improv is failing enough times that you eventually get some sense of what is good or bad. But the challenge of great improv is finding a way to quickly build any initial offer, no matter what it might be, into a rock-solid scene.

Relationships: The Bedrock of the Scene

So besides saying whatever is on the top of your head and being ready to accept your partner's offers, how else can you make a scene come together? In theory, it should only take about three lines total to establish what any given improv scene is about. It might seem daunting, but that is just to cover the basic details. You can and should add in much more information to your scene later on, but the first few lines are crucial in establishing the basic premise of the scene.

The most important thing to figure out at the very start of the scene is the *relationship* between the two characters. Naming each other in the first few lines can help a lot in this regard. If you address your scene partner as Mr. Henderson, that obviously implies something very different about your relationship than if you call your partner something like Billy or Mom.

It is a good habit to always name each other because it allows your fellow improvisers waiting in the wings to address one of the characters by name, bringing them into a subsequent scene. Still, whether you name each other or not, the first few lines should give the audience a clear sense of what relationship you and your scene partner share, how the two of you know each other, who holds the power in the relationship, and what each of you want.

Besides making a strong relationship the basis of your scene, you also need to give your scene *high stakes*. There should be a reason *why* the audience is seeing this particular scene in the character's life. Why are we being shown your character's senior prom and not his eighth birthday? The underlying reason should be that this scene we are witnessing is the single most important day in the characters' lives. That might seem like a weird idea; after all, you and your scene partner only came up with your characters a few moments ago.

The key, then, is to figure out what your character wants and then *go about getting it.* Your scene should not be the day your character thinks about telling his mom he is moving out but decides to tell her tomorrow instead. *This scene is that tomorrow,* when she finally tells her mom her plans and finds out what happens when she does.

IGP PRESENTS:
The Bullet in the Chamber

Sometimes you can be very successful when you form an idea about your character in the next scene before you step onstage. We like to call this your bullet in the chamber.

It is better that this be a loosely-formed plan, such as "I will try to play a shy character when I enter my next scene," rather than a rigid decision, such as "My next character will be unable to talk about anything other than her horrible social anxiety." The purpose behind the bullet in the chamber is to inform your behavior at the start of a scene, avoiding a completely blank slate. It can be a great fallback if everything else fails.

Bullets are a good improv spice, but as always, listen to your scene partner and be ready to forget about your idea if needed.

It is not easy to do all of that in just a few lines. It can often take a dozen or so lines to accomplish all of those objectives, and sometimes not even then. But improvisers at the absolute top of their game can really start a scene and cut to the heart of their characters' relationships in just three or four lines. That is the challenge you should set for yourself.

The Content of Your Scene: A Game

Once you have established who your characters are and what their relationship is, it is time for your scene to be *about* something.

It is important here to distinguish between *short-form* improv and *long-form* improv, as they can be very different. (More on that in Chapter Five.) In short-form improv, you "play games," with pre-specified rules. For example, one character hosts a dinner party and tries to figure out all the quirks of his guests. In long-form improv, scenes follow each other, one after the next, with little time to stop and explain to the audience what you are doing. In other words, fewer rules.

In most short-form shows, it is easy to figure out what the scene is *about*. The point of the scene is to follow the rules of the game you are playing, whether it may be speaking only in questions, incorporating pre-written lines or added props into your scene, or whatever other game you might be playing.

In long-form scenes, when you improvise without such rules, you do not have a pre-selected game to guide the scene. So then, in the absence of a specific game for the scene, what do you do?

If you are not given a game, *you make one.* In this sense, the game is more than just the rules of a scene. It is the line, the thread, that guides you, your scene partner, and the audience through the scene. To find the right game is to strike upon a rich vein of comedy, something that at its best should make improvising effortless. So what is it?

The easiest thing we could tell you is that games can be anything, absolutely anything! (Then we add an evil laugh ...) While that may be true, it is definitely not helpful. It may be better to start with an example, even if it is a silly (but true!) one:

An Immediate Gratification Player was in a scene and mimed that he was grabbing for a drink from the refrigerator. He reached a little too high, however, and suddenly, for the scene to make sense, the refrigerator had to have been ten feet tall. This seemingly innocuous act got a huge response from the audience. After that point, *every subsequent line in the scene was punctuated with another huge refrigerator door being opened.* By the end of the scene, there were at least two-dozen giant fridges somewhere in that kitchen.

That, believe it or not, is an example of a *game.* It may be even harder to believe that the audience absolutely loved it.

Games can, and probably should, be a little more sophisticated than that. But the game usually is a great answer to the question: "What is funny about this scene?" Or, an even easier question: "What is *different* about this scene?"

Perhaps a son has come home to tell his dad he is going to pursue his dreams to become a rock star. The father might reveal that he himself was once a world-famous rock star, and he wants to save his son from making the same mistakes he did. Already, this scene has a clear *relationship* and obvious *high stakes.* Now, the game: the dad does not just want to save his son from the horrors of rock stardom, he wants to save him from the horrors of *everything.* The son might say he still plans to finish school, and the father grows even more horrified at the idea of education. The kid might threaten to walk out the door, at which point the dad recoils at the past horror of doors. Take the stakes and *amplify* them, and a basic game comes through.

That is one possible game. Here, briefly, is another possibility. In that original line, the father does not just mention he was a rock star, he says he was *world-famous.* The son might become frustrated with this, exclaiming his dad always outdoes him at everything. He might talk about the time he performed in the school play the same night his dad opened the biggest smash in Broadway history or the time his little league team lost the championship at the very moment his dad hit a home run to win the World Series. The scene could then end with the father one-upping his son once more. Again, you take the first bit of information (father is like son, but better) and amplify it.

Even a third possibility for the game comes from the fact that the dad was a world-famous rock star and yet, somehow, his son never knew. What else does the son not know about his father? Every subsequent statement the dad makes could be prefaced by "I know you'll find this hard to believe," or "Son, I have something to tell you," followed by a series of increasingly dull, unsurprising revelations. In this version of the game, you build expectations and then do the opposite, like "Dad, what do you mean you're left-handed?"

You might notice a certain commonality to these games — they all seem a little absurd. This shift toward the crazy in an improv scene is known as the *tilt*. The name itself is well chosen, because it evokes something that pushes a scene away from normalcy without knocking it all the way over. You do not want to instantly jump from a down-to-earth, gritty scene about siblings reconnecting after twenty years apart straight to a mystical quest of dragon warriors fighting for the jewel of Baldurash on behalf of the Phalanx of Gilgamoth. At least put in a couple of intermediary steps before going somewhere that crazy!

Tilts work because they are still somewhat credible; an audience can still believe in what you are doing. Tilts also work well in the context of games because they take the premise of the game and stretch it to its breaking point. The tilt is not license to go utterly insane. Rather, it is a way to throw some minor point of discordance into high relief, to blow up something vaguely amusing until it is completely hilarious.

Indeed, that is what all the games we have mentioned pick up on. Simple as it was, the refrigerator game worked because it responded to the audience's surprise and amusement at an absurd physical element being added to the scene. The three games spinning out of the rock star scene all build off of something unusual about the father's statement, whether it is the severity of his concern for his son, the fact that he used to be extraordinarily good at rocking, or that his son somehow had no idea of this extremely noteworthy part of his dad's past. None of these are funny on their own terms. Instead, they are moments of incongruity, exactly the sort of thing that will pop up when two people are making up a scene together on the spot.

Some of the stuff you do in a scene will not make complete sense. That is not a bad thing at all. Rather, that is the key to finding games. If you listen carefully, find the oddities, and turn enough of them into games, you will have one seriously awesome show on your hands. That, in its essence, is the structure of every improv scene that does not already have a game associated with it.

Still, there is more to work than simply building a relationship and finding a game. Let's now look at a few more advanced wrinkles you can throw into your scenes.

Knowing Your Space: Performing Physically in Scenes

A lot of people try improv simply because they want to make people laugh. They may not have prior experience as a performer. Whenever you improvise in a scene, whether it is part of a show or just practice, you always want to have a sense of how you are presenting yourself visually. You could be hilarious, and people would not enjoy your comedy fully because it is not presented well.

For instance, are you making eye contact with your scene partner? Many improvisers have a tendency to look anywhere *except* at their scene partner. This generally hurts the reality of the scene, particularly if you are making eye contact with the audience instead. Unless your character has a specific reason to look away — perhaps he or she is unusually timid — you should not be afraid to make and maintain eye contact with your scene partner.

You should also consider your movement through the space. Some improvisers walk around a lot, particularly if they are launching into longer lines of dialogue. That is fine, but make sure there is some sort of motivation for your movement and that you are not just pacing. Random pacing generally just looks like random pacing to the audience, and it can be fairly distracting.

Related to this is a concept known as "the improvisers' three feet," which is a tendency for scene partners to maintain about three feet of distance — no more, no less — between each other at all times. You should not be afraid to get physically close to each other if that is what the scene demands, nor should you be afraid to explore the entire space, particularly if you are on a relatively large stage. Varying the distance between scene partners might seem not particularly important, but you will be amazed how much of what you do in a scene is informed by your basic physical interactions and how much of an effect varying them even a little can have.

IGP PRESENTS:
When Good Scenes Go Bad and How to Save Them

Good scenes can go bad in a number of different ways. Your scene can devolve into unfunny arguing, for example, or perhaps you are stricken by a terrible case of onstage giggles. These are highly contagious.

If things start to feel as though they are spiraling out of control, remember that the show must go on. Stay in character, and explain your bickering or laughter in the context of the scene's reality. For example, "I'm sorry, Sorcerer Dave, your wizard's hat is making me laugh."

Focus on your relationship in the scene, and try to move the scene along by making tough choices based on it. Ultimately, when a scene really goes bad, it needs to be ended by other improvisers in your troupe, but it is your job to do the best you can until they edit the scene.

Going for the Gusto: Adding Extra Characters

So far, we have discussed basic scenes with two characters. In our experience, those are the most successful, and we think sticking to a two-character scene often works best. On occasion, however, someone may feel the need to add themselves to a scene you are in, or perhaps you will decide that a scene you are not in would be kicked up another notch of hilarity if you enter as a third character.

Although two-person scenes may be the default, there is plenty of room for the addition of extra characters. But it is a relatively advanced maneuver and one that takes a bit of thought and practice if it is to be exploited to its full potential. There are two basic factors to consider: why an extra character (or characters) should be added and how more than two characters can interact in a single scene without devolving into chaos. It is a lot easier for three people to talk over each other than for two.

Let's start with the *why*. There are two basic reasons why you might choose to enter a scene as a third character. The worst-case scenario is that a scene is failing and there is no clear way to end it, so the third character is basically a last-ditch effort to save the scene. In IGP's experience, that is a pretty rare occurrence. It is something we have maybe experienced once or twice in a year of doing shows, so it is not worth practicing. You are basically predicting yourself to fail.

Ideally, an extra character allows the primary relationship of the scene to be thrown into *sharper focus,* to better clarify how the two characters see each other by revealing how they view the third. As an example, imagine a scene where a mother and son are fighting over his curfew time. How might the addition of a third character help reveal new facets of that relationship? Let's say the father enters the scene. Depending on the side he takes in the argument, the audience learns something about the dynamics of the family and how they tend to settle disputes. Or perhaps this third character is the son's perfect younger sister, who can stay up as late as she wants because, well, she is *perfect.* That helps the audience better understand the nature of the relationship between the mother and the son while adding a third character who is funny in his or her own right.

But it can be easy to go overboard with a third character. By entering an established scenario, the improviser playing the third character often has a readymade setup for a great joke. If two old schoolmates at their twentieth reunion mention their crazy old shop teacher Mr. Hanson, then what could possibly be funnier than Mr. Hanson showing up out of nowhere? Such an addition can easily get laughs, but if the entire point of the character is that Mr. Hanson is hilariously eccentric, then it is questionable how much this third character really tells us about the relationship between the two classmates. Additionally, once the surprise wears off, Mr. Hanson will have a tough time supporting the initial scene partners in whatever game they were playing.

You should use extra characters to complement existing scenes and not use those scenes as glorified introductions for your grand entrance as someone quirky. But do not be afraid of adding yourself as an extra character. For one thing, varying up the number of characters in scenes is a great way to keep the audience engaged. But if you find yourself constantly entering scenes as a third character, you may want to stop yourself the next time you get the urge to add yourself to a scene and simply ask, "What is the point of this character? What does this character add to the current scene?" Keeping those questions in mind should provide you all the guidance you need to judge whether you ought to enter a scene as an extra character.

Now, once a third (or a fourth or fifth) character is added, what is a scene supposed to do with so many people? Having that many people in a scene places an even greater burden on *listening* to your scene partners and giving everyone a chance to contribute so that the scene does not become chaotic. Even so, it can be tricky to juggle three or more characters in a scene even if everyone involved is trying their hardest to make it work, so one common trick is to collapse and combine the perspectives and motivations of the various characters so that there are still only two sides to the scene.

Let's explain what we mean here by returning to the curfew scene with the mother and son. If a third improviser enters as the father, he might agree with the mother (in our real-life experience, the most probable outcome *by far*) and support her in the argument with her son. In this way, the scene is still essentially two-sided, with the son on one side and the parents on the other. All the other permutations are certainly possible. The father might agree with the son, or perhaps the mother and son decide to team up to convince the father of something. But the basic point is that the third character is added in such a way that he or she complements the other characters and merely modifies the existing relationship, not morphs it completely.

It can also be fun to have these allegiances change over the course of the scene. Perhaps the father initially agrees with the mother, but when she also plans on sending their son to the army, he starts to have second thoughts. The audience enjoys seeing his internal struggle: he sympathizes with the son but feels obligated to support his wife.

That, in the end, is the responsibility of any third character — you have to add something to the scene you are entering. Otherwise you might as well just start a new scene.

IGP PRESENTS:
A Third Character – Seen, Not Heard

Sometimes third characters are most effective when they are like a Victorian child, seen and not heard. Often, a third character's entrance and dialogue can interrupt the momentum of the improvisers already onstage, but you can still add a great deal to a scene without saying a single line!

During one IGP show, there was a great scene between two jewel thieves who had a very specific, silent physicality for sneaking into bank vaults and jewelry stores. Later in the show, when a man proposed to his girlfriend, the two jewel thieves silently entered the scene, performing their stealth physicality. They did not interrupt the scene, allowing the couple to continue their romantic moment, but they got a huge laugh because the audience knew they were coming to steal the ring.

Contributions can be smaller, as well. Perhaps you are just entering to help to better define the space for the performers, for example, by showing that there is a lake by skipping stones on it. Whatever you do, remember that you do not have to speak to effectively add to the scene.

All Good Scenes Must Come to an End

If you are wondering exactly how to switch from one scene to the next, it is simple. If it is a short-form game you are ending, step in front of the improvisers and yell something obvious, for example, "And scene!" If it is a long-form scene that you want to end, step in front of the improvisers, clearly break up the space they were operating in with your body, and simply begin a new scene. (More on the mechanics of this in Chapter Nine.)

Better than the question of how is the question of *when.* Finding the right moment to end an improv scene, whether you are waiting in the wings in a long-form show looking for the right moment to edit and start fresh or if you are running a short-form game and looking for the perfect final line, is one of the trickiest, most intuitive parts of the improv process. There is no easy way to explain how it is done. Still, since we live to serve (and we did have the gall to actually write a book on how to do improv, so we really ought to offer you something), we can provide some basic guidelines for how to find the right moment to end a scene.

The most useful concept here is that of the *beat.* Other improvisers may use this term to mean something completely different, but in IGP lingo, a beat is a moment in the scene that somehow stands out from those that came before it. A beat might be a particularly hilarious line, a callback to the start of the scene, a shocking twist (which often leaves the scene with nowhere left to go), or something that feels like the natural culmination of the game that the improvisers have been playing.

In shows, beats are relatively easy to pick out. If a scene gets a huge laugh from the audience, then that is a beat. You always want to edit on a beat, but you do not have to edit on *every* beat. If the first big laugh comes thirty seconds into a scene, you probably will want to let the scene continue a little while longer and juice that laugh lemon for some funny lemonade. Every rule has its exceptions, of course. If the previous few scenes were quite long or the laugh was particularly massive, you could consider cutting the scene right then and there. Of course, stopping people when they are successful does not always make them happy.

Finding a beat is difficult to practice because it is one of the few things that is actually much easier to do in a show. When you are just practicing in a group, you are highly unlikely to get the same sort of huge reactions from others as you will from an audience. Plus, improv troupes tend to laugh at different things than improv audiences because improvisers tend to have weird senses of humor. (But hey, that is why we do improv and not therapy!)

This is a skill that you can best develop by simply paying close attention, which is something you should be doing anyway, of course. You can start to build up an intuitive sense of what sort of lines and moments are good beats. Your first few shows in particular are a great time to develop this skill.

You can also think about beats in terms of their place in the overall arc of a scene. If we can bust out some old information from middle school English class, all works of fiction are supposed to have *exposition,* which sets up what the story is about, *rising action,* which builds up the conflict, the *climax,* which as far as we remember just means "turning point," the *falling action,* which resolves the conflict, and the *denouement,* which is pretty much just the conclusion. (Potentially interesting note: this chart is actually called Freytag's Pyramid, after nineteenth century German writer Gustav Freytag, and it is apparently a pretty big deal in literary theory. Who knew?)

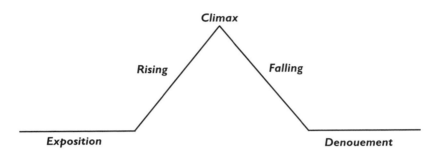

In this model, the first couple of lines in an improv scene serve as the exposition, setting up the relationship and the setting. The game that the improvisers find is the rising action. The beat is the climax, the point of absolute greatest tension in the scene. In this case, "point of absolute greatest tension" is code for "point of absolute greatest comedy." Improv scenes, as a rule, do not have falling actions or denouements, mostly because they are not particularly funny or necessary. Of course, the fact that they are generally unfunny is a major reason why they are unnecessary. Improvisational *comedy* is all about the laughs, after all. So really all you need to do to find the beat of a scene is to find the climax and then edit. Simple, right?

Not so fast, my friend. The problem is that it is possible for a scene to have lots of moments that really, really look like climaxes but are not. Showing the type of originality you would expect from the creative class, these moments are called "false climaxes" or anticlimaxes, which appear to represent a turning point in the scene but are actually not quite important enough to count. *Hamlet,* often considered the greatest work in the history of English literature, could be considered nothing more than a series of anticlimaxes followed by a graveyard and a swordfight. Spoiler alert! In much the same way, you need to make sure you do not edit on the wrong beat.

If you edit too soon before the scene has really built toward a real climax, the audience might feel shortchanged, as though they never really got to understand what the scene was about. If you let it go too far beyond what was, in retrospect, the obvious climax of the scene, then you are past the point of maximum interest. A dead giveaway that a scene has gone on too long is if one of the improvisers pauses, as though searching for *anything* to say, and then starts a sentence with, "So..." At that point, he or she is starting a new conversation, and if that is going to happen, you might as well start a new scene as well.

Obviously, this is a tricky art. But do not despair! Whether you are editing at a beat or missing by a mile, the best antidote to a poorly timed edit is a *good next scene*. Audiences might remember a clumsy edit, but they are much, much more likely to remember all the laughs they had in the scenes on either side of it.

When you are editing correctly, no one should even notice you are doing anything at all. Well, they should probably notice a new scene has started, but you get the idea. Additionally, wherever a beat in a scene might be, it is never, ever in the middle of somebody's line. Edits that come mid-sentence are about the clumsiest, most jarring ones there are, but they are also the simplest to avoid. We will get more into the specific mechanics of editing later on, but in the end, if you can keep these points in mind, you and your troupe will be just fine.

All You Need Is Trust (Love Is OK, Too)

If improv shows are all about their scenes, then scenes are all about *trust*. There are many kinds of trust: trust between scene partners to accept each other's offers and build a scene together; trust in your abilities to find the game of the scene without forcing it; trust in the audience to follow you into more absurd territory when you tilt the scene; and trust in the rest of the troupe to end the scene when the time is right.

Much like bungee jumping and unlike poker, improvisational comedy simply does not work without trust. That is not all there is to it — there are still ten chapters left, after all — but it is pretty fundamental to the success of your scenes.

In the next chapter, we will go beyond the group dynamics of a scene to discuss how *you can behave* in a scene to make it even more successful. Never forget that as go your improv scenes, so goes your improv show.

Chapter Three

To Do or Not to Do: The Rules of Improv

After days of waiting, the improvisers at the bottom of the mountain looked up to see their improv king descend with two stone tablets. "Have you brought down the rules of improv?" the people asked as they eagerly eyed the stones.

The improv king responded: "Don't you know you're not supposed to ask questions in improv?" And with that, he angrily smashed the tablets. "Now there are no rules," he said.

The improvisers looked at each other. "This doesn't really make sense," they said. "No, it doesn't," the king replied with a nod. Then he looked out into the distance. "If only IGP could explain it ... "

By now, you should have a fair idea of what an improv scene is all about. This chapter consists of tips for how you can make your improv scenes even better.

This chapter could just be of a list of traditional dos and don'ts for improvisational comedy. But, in IGP's experience, there have been many times when we did and failed. There also have been times when we did not and succeeded.

Yes, there are certain, much-discussed, overarching rules to improvisational comedy. If more experienced improvisers see you break these rules, they will more likely than not roll their eyes, say "tsk tsk," and do a third pretentious thing. But because it is important that you are at least aware of the rules, this chapter will list them out for you.

But it is also important to realize that you can be very successful breaking rules and very unsuccessful following them. Consider rules to be more like guidelines. They can be informative, but they should not bar you from doing something that could still be very funny and develop the scene.

With each rule listed in this chapter, IGP will explain the thought behind it and tell you when you can break it. So read on, you rulebreaker, you.

Rule 1: Don't Say "No"

"Hey, isn't that a double negative? Doesn't that just mean I should say yes?" On the contrary, not saying no is an important rule all by itself.

The Thought behind It

When you and your scene partner improvise onstage, you are trying to *establish a reality* for the audience. In any given scene, you could be bank robbers who have just stolen a baby or schoolteachers fighting over recess rules. The audience will accept this reality because you told them (and showed them) that is what you were doing. Often onstage, when you say no to what someone says, you are denying the reality.

For example, the statements "No, we didn't just rob this bank" or "No, we're not schoolteachers anymore" strongly break the reality you have established. This kills the momentum of the scene and forces your partner to shift directions. Your partner will also lose trust in you. If you deny your partner's ideas by saying no, he or she will be less likely to offer up strong ideas in the future.

Some people in improv talk about a "block." This can be a verb or a noun. When someone blocks you, that person is negating your reality. This can often be because the person said no. But someone can demonstrate a block in more subtle ways. Perhaps you make a suggestion in a scene ("Let's eat some steak") and your partner just changes the subject ("I need to talk about my birthday"). This negation can be very frustrating for improvisers, and it often turns your scenes into ones based around unproductive conflict. This can be fun at first, but tedious after some time ("No! Yes! No! Yes ... no!"). If you block someone, he or she will come to think of you as a bad scene partner.

When It Might Be OK to Break the Rule

If you can get the hang of it, the word "no" can be a part of your improv toolkit. You just need to wield it appropriately. Sometimes denial can be playful. You can use the word "no" to be coy. If your partner asks, "Did you steal my cookie?" and you respond, "Noooo," instantly the audience and your scene partner know that you *did* steal the cookie but are pretending you did not. If you do it right, "no" can be a way to say "yes."

IGP Presents:
No, No, No!

The easiest way to block someone is to say the word "no." But there are other ways to be "blocky." Here are a few things you could say:

I don't think so.

Let's not talk about it.

Let's do something different.

That's not technically true.

We're sailors! (when the other person has just said you are bankers)

We're bankers! (when the other person has just said you are sailors)

I would help you, but I'm glued to the floor. Oh, no, looks like you just stepped in it, too!

I'm not going to talk until you leave.

It's hard to be friends with you because you don't speak English.

You want to dance? Oh, I can't dance.

Hey, you and I should dance! Oh wait, I have no shoes.

No, don't shoot my son. Actually, wait, go ahead and shoot him. (removes the danger from the scene)

I'm confused as to why you're talking because I just removed your mouth.

Rule 2: Say, "Yes, and!"

Often, if people know one thing about improv, they know "Yes, and!" We in IGP have heard people say, "Oh, improv, that's just yes, and, right?" If you search for "Yes, and!" on the Internet (or whatever shadowy search device you are using now in the twenty-second century), improv-related articles are the first results to appear. This two-word catchphrase will not automatically make you very funny. It *can* make you a parrot, but that is not the primary goal of this book. Nonetheless, "Yes, and!" is an important improv concept that will help you work collaboratively with your scene partner to build a scene.

The Thought behind It

The key to this rule is the concept of *acceptance,* which we touched on in the last chapter. If someone onstage gives you an offer, for example, that you are riding a tandem bicycle, you accept it (*yes*) and then you build on it (*and*) perhaps by announcing that this is the perfect first date. The first person can then add again (*and*), this time by saying that he hopes she does not mind how much he sweats. There, in just three lines using "Yes, and," the partners have established a first date scene in which the girl is slowly becoming turned off by her date's perspiration.

If your partner does not feel that you are accepting offers, he or she might become more timid and less likely to offer anything in the future. It is thus incredibly important to listen to your scene partner so that you can hear the offers being given.

The best improvisers are the best scene partners — people who support the other performers onstage. The best way to be supportive is to accept what you are given and then to add to it.

When It Might Be OK to Break the Rule

If you really are not confident in your partner's offers (perhaps they are offensive or incomprehensible), it might be fine to say, "No, but." You can deny a partner's offer and build something in another direction. Then later, offstage, apologize for blocking your partner, and explain why you did it. Say: "I'm sorry, Steve, but I didn't think that I should be a cancer patient, so I decided to be magically healed." The more open you are about why you refuse to say "Yes, and!" the more a partner will trust you onstage.

Rule 3: Don't Kill Your Scene Partner

This one is simple. A one-person scene is very sad to watch and difficult to perform. Do not eliminate your partner onstage.

The Thought behind It

While death can be funny for a brief second, it is also a big block. It forces your scene partners to crawl on the floor and to shut their mouths. This breaks other rules, for example, that scene partners should not be silent and that you should be accepting of offers. A killing is a big refusal of your scene partner's right to improvise.

When It Might Be OK to Break the Rule

Sometimes a long scene is building up to a death. Killing should not be completely forbidden. If audience members knew that no scene partner could ever die, the dramatic tension behind a threat of murder would cease to exist. So it can be OK to die onstage.

Additionally, if someone comes on as a third character just to be killed, that is an OK use of the improvised murder. As long as you leave two people onstage to talk to each other and the third person does not feel that his or her ideas were rejected, murder is OK. (Note to IGP's lawyers: Murder is *not* OK.)

Rule 4: Don't Ask Questions

This is another rule you will hear on the first day of Improv University. Questions are not evil, but they can hurt a scene in several ways. As a beginning improviser, it is best to avoid them. You can then work them back into the conversation as you improve your game.

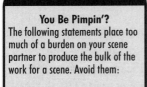

You Be Pimpin'?
The following statements place too much of a burden on your scene partner to produce the bulk of the work for a scene. Avoid them:

You're getting a call from someone.
What's that you're carrying?
I wrote you a poem. Read it aloud.
Here's a present. Open it and tell me what it is.
Where were you on August fifth?
What are you doing right now?

The Thought behind It

When you ask a question of a scene partner, often you are asking them to produce information that does not yet exist. A question like "What am I doing?" does many things: it reinforces to the audience that you do not know what you are doing, it requires your scene partner to produce an entertaining and credible answer, and it generally shifts the burden of the scene away from the asker of the question.

Perhaps if whoever is being asked the question onstage is the most hilarious person alive, perhaps if you have been given the opportunity to improvise with a famous comedian, perhaps if your scene partner is incredibly clever, it will not matter whether or not you ask him or her a question. That person is capable enough to give a great answer. But for most people, it can be very annoying and stressful to receive a question onstage and be forced to come up with a great answer.

Generally, questions or other actions like it — things that require your partner to produce the bulk of the information — are called *pimps*.

When you *pimp* someone, you are making that person do the bulk of the work onstage. Instead of asking a question, provide the answer. Rather than asking "Who are you?" say, "So I presume you are Dr. Sanchez. I didn't expect to find you here." This gives your partner something to work from, while he or she still can decide some of the details, for example, why Dr. Sanchez is there. (But who can predict Dr. Sanchez?)

When It Might Be OK to Break the Rule

If you really trust your partner and feel that you communicate well with him or her, questions can really add to a scene. In general, the best questions onstage are not quiz questions. Instead, they are statements in the form of a question. "What do you think you are doing here?" for example really means "You are not welcome here." A rhetorical question like "Why don't you love me?" does not necessarily need an answer and thus is not a pimp. If someone tells you "Improv means never asking a question," that person is not living up to his or her improv potential. Questions can make a scene great.

Rule 5: Listen. Listen. Listen.

Too often onstage offers are given and then ignored because they were not heard. It can be easy to focus on yourself while improvising, to worry about what you will say or do next. Listening is incredibly important. If you do not listen, audience members will, and they will call you out on it.

The Thought behind It

Clumsy improvisers who do not listen to their scene partners make easy mistakes. They get names wrong, they forget where they are, and they change the relationship. Scenes can quickly become incoherent if too many offers are being thrown out and not accepted. Thus, it is important to stay focused on what is happening around you.

This rule could be more broadly termed as *pay attention*. In addition to listening, you should be focusing on body language, expressions, and other nonverbal cues to understand what your scene partner is trying to convey.

Use your ears offstage as well. If a scene is great, listen to the key details so you can revisit that scene later in the show. Clever callbacks to previous moments or jokes in a show can be very gratifying for the audience, as they will feel that *they* are being rewarded for listening and thus will pay more attention. In order to do this, it is important that you listen as well.

When It Might Be OK to Break the Rule

It is never OK not to listen. Always listen, unless your character is clueless and incompetent. In that case, listen anyway and pretend that you did not.

Rule 6: Don't Be Silent

Performing improvised comedy onstage is largely about words. What you do is very important, but what you say can often seal the deal for audience members, causing them to quote you on the ride home. So speak up! Use your words!

The Thought behind It

It can be easy to stand around and mime a funny action, waiting for your partner to speak. But if your partner has the same mentality, soon there will be two people onstage with nothing to say. Fill the silence. Too often scene partners are worried about what to say, whether it will be funny or not. The least funny thing you can do is be silent onstage, staring at your partner. If you do not say anything, the audience will have huge expectations for when you finally do speak.

When It Might Be OK to Break the Rule

A well-placed pause can light up a scene, add tension, and give you time to breathe. These are often most effective once you have let your scene develop. If you think it is time to let your actions speak for your words, make sure those actions are entertaining.

Rule 7: Don't Use Just Words

Actions, in improv, can be just as loud as words. It is not enough to have a fast mouth; your body has to move in improv as well. So do not make all your scenes just talking. It can be very boring from the perspective of an audience member to watch two people talk to each other. Be physical onstage.

The Thought behind It

Physicality onstage is not only visually interesting, it can be hilarious. It avoids the monotony of dialogue alone and spices up scenes.

Thus, it is always better onstage to add some action to your dialogue. Pick up a wrench and fix a faucet. Chop up some carrots for a stew. Wash dishes or take a shower. Rock climb or roller-skate. Shave a cow! This gives your audience something to watch and it often informs your character. A babysitter fixing a faucet is much different from a babysitter standing around and talking.

When It Might Be OK to Break the Rule

Adding action to a scene is usually a positive thing. You do not want to add too much action to a scene, however. If your son is trying to tell you something and you are frantically operating a very complex loom to create a scarf, sometimes action can distract from the scene (although it could be very funny). Also, do not use physicality to break the physical reality that others have created. Do not dance through a table others have set up unless it is purposeful. Be careful not to overdo it.

Rule 8: Don't Just Be Witty

When you do use your words, be careful not to try to make every single word funny. This can slow down a scene and infuriate a partner. While an audience might be gratified at first, if the scene does not go anywhere, you may find that your wit will dry up.

The Thought behind It

First, it should be said that not everyone has the skills to be able to break this rule. Crafting hilarious dialogue on the spot is a tall order — many people in IGP cannot do it. But that is fine because that is not what improvised comedy is about. The focus should be on strong relationships, raised stakes, and everything this book is about. If improv were just about being witty, this book would be two words long. (The first word would be the word *be*.)

Often, a witty scene partner, while entertaining, can take away from what the scene is really about. When every line is aiming for chuckles, relationships start to disappear, and the stakes start to dissolve. Jokey dialogue can also disrupt the reality of a scene, making it more implausible. It can often serve as a distraction.

Also, constant wittiness is often at the expense of your scene partner. He or she has been busy working to build an interesting scene and forward the conflict, but if you are just concerned with making jokes, you'll disrupt the scene's momentum and alienate your scene partner who has been doing unappreciated, high-quality improv.

Of course, this is not to say that your scenes should not be funny — this book is about improv comedy after all. What we are trying to stress is that the comedy should come from the development of scenes. If executed properly, the scene will provide you with opportunities to be funny and witty so you do not have to force it.

If you really do have an irrepressible wit, congratulations! Maybe you have a future at stand-up comedy. Or dinner parties.

When It Might Be OK to Break the Rule

The idea of not *just* being witty is a pretty safe rule of thumb. But be sure to let your wit seep through if you have it. The audience will love you for it.

Rule 9: Focus on Relationships

As we said in the previous chapter, relationships are the backbone to a successful improv scene. It can be very helpful to audience members to know how two improvisers know each other and how they feel about each other. Cultivating a strong relationship at the start of a scene will pay off big by the end.

The Thought behind It

Starting a scene with a strong relationship can save time. You can skip past the getting-to-know-each-other phase and the first-encounter scenes. These are the scenes where you and your scene partner figure out who the other person is over the course of the scene. These are not inherently bad, but they have a tendency to get old quickly.

It does not take much to establish a strong relationship right off of the bat. One statement can do it. Examples include: "Ma, not again;" "I like your thinking, Jenkins;" "Great game, Coach." Using a statement that automatically defines a relationship advances your scene straight into the action. This makes it more exciting to watch.

When It Might Be OK to Break the Rule

If you have a clever idea for a "first meeting" scene that you want to try, have at it! If you do so, focus on defining the relationship quickly. This will only help you and your scene partner find the funny of the scene.

Rule 10: Maintain the Reality

You want your audience to buy in to what you are doing, to believe what they see is real. To keep up the illusion, it is extremely important for you to believe in your reality.

The Thought behind It

The audience's hold on reality in an improvised performance can be very shaky. You are first asking them to believe that every scene is in a different location and that every time you appear onstage you are a different character. These are huge leaps of faith for an audience member, and you need to make those jumps as easy as possible.

Think of the reality as a precious object that you do not want to break, a lot like your own mother or the urn that you keep your dog in. There are a few key aspects of the scene that help maintain the reality.

First, as we discussed in the previous chapter, you must respect the physical space. If someone is pretending that he or she is washing a car, you should not walk through the car. When someone turns the stage into a hotel room, you should not turn it into a bar in the same scene. This is again about accepting offers, extending the concept of "Yes, and!" to the physical space that your partner defines.

Improv allows you the freedom to create any sort of physical space onstage. In order for the audience to believe you are in a Jacuzzi, you must respect the physical laws that define a Jacuzzi. Adjust your physicality to match your surroundings.

If your partner hands you a glass of champagne and you let go of it without acknowledging that it dropped, your body is telling the audience that the glass never existed, that it was fake. Be hyperaware of the physical environment you and your scene partners create and be consistent with it.

As an improviser, you can make character choices that make these bizarre physical spaces all the more real and true to the audience. If you are in a champagne-filled Jacuzzi on a Grecian isle, you might choose to play a honeymooning couple, two vacationing senior citizens, or a couple of Jacuzzi repairmen who hit it big. Creating and maintaining strong characters allows the audience to believe that you are real people in a real world, however crazy it might seem.

When It Might Be OK to Break the Rule

When you have established a well-defined world onstage, it sometimes works to modify this reality. As long as you are consistent and acknowledge these changes, the audience will be onboard.

If in a scene you and your partner are detectives on the hunt, you might dash across the stage to signify the passage of time or the changing of the location. You can defy the laws of physics and make that part of your new reality as long as you create consistent rules. Do not take these decisions for granted!

Rule 11: Vary It Up

Variety, within scenes and between scenes, is key in improv. You want to show the audience a range of emotions and characters and give them everything you have onstage.

The Thought behind It

An audience will be more excited by variety, by seeing different types of improvisers do different types of things. The more range you can display, the better.

This means differentiating yourself from a scene partner by playing a different kind of character. If your partner is an English butler, you certainly could have a successful scene by joining him as a second English butler. But if you want to vary things up, you might play a thief raiding the English butler's mansion.

Vary your characters between scenes. If you are a high school heartthrob in one scene, be a mad scientist in the next. You will have more fun by playing different characters, and your audience will enjoy watching you test your improv range. Play with different emotions in different scenes. Even within a scene, it can help to shift emotions. The audience will be intrigued if you start a scene angry and grow sad much more so than if you start angry and stay angry.

Mix it up. Be your own DJ and play a few new songs along with the hits.

When It Might Be OK to Break the Rule

If a scene or character works well, it can be fun to bring it back later on in an improv show as a callback. This can be overdone, however, and if a character stays around for too long, the audience can grow tired. But, within reason, it can be a great idea to return to a winning concept.

IGP Presents:
Pop Culture and Vulgarity

Nothing here states that you cannot be vulgar onstage, although we in IGP avoid it as a rule. That is what we have decided works for our audience, but you may have a different kind of population you serve, one that craves obscenity.

The same thing goes for pop culture references. We do not include it in our improv because we think it is too easy. Our audiences, however, do request it. IGP did four shows the week after the hit movie Avatar came out, and the suggestion "Pandora" was probably yelled out one hundred times.

Often, pop culture references can leave some people who are less knowledgeable out of the joke. We will have more to say about pop culture and vulgarity later. For now, just know that IGP avoids it, though you are free to write your own rules in that regard.

Rule 12: Don't Think! Have Fun! Don't Worry!

The minute you start to focus on the rules is the same minute you stop being funny. Most of these rules are easy enough to follow, but you should not put following them over the joy of improvising. If you begin to kick yourself every time you ask a question, you will lose some natural spontaneity. And then improvising will be that much harder.

Practice so that you internalize these rules. That way, when you perform, you do not have to think about these techniques. Instead, you can focus entirely on your scene and scene partner.

The Thought behind It

Improv is fun. So have fun. There is not a lot to it.

When It Might Be OK to Break the Rule

Maybe you are very depressed, and life has no joy for you. In that case, seek professional help. Or channel that pain into your improv. It might be really funny.

Are Rules Important?

So those are the rules. The rules! The rules!

Here is the biggest tip: The best way you can follow these rules is to break them. They really are only guidelines to improvised comedy. They cannot make or break you, and IGP has had its share of joyous rule infractions over the years. In one scene, an IGP member was given an offer and then screamed "No!" If that does not show a hilarious disregard of the rules, then not much else can.

So take all these rules with a grain of salt. You may wonder to yourself: "If I follow these steps, will my improv be funny?" It really is not as easy as that. If you follow these rules, you will definitely be a competent improviser. And if you are doing it right and you have a good scene partner, it should be funny. But in the end, some scenes just will not work. After all, there are not any rules forcing audience members to laugh. But if you follow these rules, it is definitely more likely.

OKAY, UP NEXT...
TWENTY LAPS
AROUND THE FIELD,
FIFTY-YARD
SPRINTS, THEN
BEAR CRAWLS.

YES, AND?

Chapter Four
DRILL TO THE CORE: PRACTICING IMPROV

Maybe you were born under funny stars. And maybe you think practicing improv comedy, of all things, is for chumps. Because how can you practice something that does not have a script and is never predetermined?

Simply put, improvisers who practice are better (read: funnier) than the ones who do not. The Immediate Gratification Players practice four hours a week, not to mention the countless hours we spend in the weight room. We always feel more confident in our skills after a practice session and confident in our bodies after a trip to the gym.

So you want to get better at improv? The best comedians got to where they are by trying things out. A lot. Put down the book and give it a go ...

Why practice? Name your favorite athletes, musicians, or reality TV stars. They got to where they are today because of practice. While many people are naturally funny, a great improviser is someone who puts in the work to develop a strong skill set and improv mentality, both on their own and with their troupe.

Much like with sports, you have to be in great improv shape to perform well during a show. Even if you are an incredibly funny person, you will be rusty and unprepared to hit one out of the park if you have not practiced. You also want to be in good shape for your scene partners. No one wants to do a scene with an improv *fatty!* Setting up a regular practice schedule with your troupe and staying focused during practice time will lead to great results. Essentially, the more improv you do, the better.

In this chapter we will talk about running a practice and different drills you can use to bulk up your improv muscles. Especially if you have little performance experience, an extensive practice schedule can get you in great shape for performing in an improv show. Drilling to find your strengths and address your weaknesses can be incredibly rewarding when you see the progress you are making together.

Practice will not always be easy. You want to challenge yourself in areas of difficulty and be able to take constructive criticism well. Luckily for you, after a really long and hard improv practice, you will only be out of breath from laughing. (We are not athletes.)

Staying in Shape: Your Practice Approach

First and foremost, your troupe should meet regularly for practice. At the beginning of the year (or each semester if you are in school), make sure to meet and set up a weekly schedule of one or two practices a week. The Immediate Gratification Players practice twice a week for two hours each. However, we have heard of other college troupes who practice as much as three hours a day or as little as one hour a week.

The important thing is to maintain a consistent schedule that works for everyone. If possible, try to also meet in the same practice space or set of spaces. Keeping a routine is important so you can spend more time focusing on improv and less time stressing about when and where the next practice is taking place.

Attitude is as essential to practice as space and time. Approaching practice with the right mentality is incredibly important. Whether you are a leader of your troupe or just another member, work to establish right from the beginning that *everyone in the troupe is funny.* Receiving comedy critiques can be difficult, as they can feel very personal. Being funny makes up a large part of many people's identities — think of the very title of this book. Being told that a scene you did was not working or was not funny can feel like an affront to your personality.

That is why it is so vital to have a group understanding that everyone knows that everyone else is funny. It helps to remember that maybe you all made it through the same audition process, or perhaps you chose each other as improv partners. There must be a reason you are all in the same room.

Practice is only there to help you get better. Accepting as fact that everyone is funny provides the foundation for giving and receiving criticism so you can really start to improve. With a strong, cohesive group mentality, practice becomes incredibly satisfying as you can see yourself getting better.

Keeping it Together: Running Practice

Most likely the leader of the troupe will be in charge of running and directing practices. Often professional troupes will have a director or coach (sometimes paid) who works with the group and does not perform. For many groups, however, the person running practice will also be a performer and member of the troupe, which, while fun, brings its own unique set of challenges. Think of a general who fights alongside his men versus one who oversees the battle from the war room and maybe stays in his pajamas.

Managing improvisers and getting them to focus is about as easy as herding cats — cats who all are very funny and do not like to be herded. There are a number of things you can do to keep practices on track and productive. Come prepared with a plan of how each practice will go to ensure the troupe stays on task and engaged. Try to budget time either before or after practice to hang out and socialize.

When we practice, we routinely start to improvise ten minutes into our first hour once everyone has had time to hang out and catch up. We will also often eat meals together after practice. While there will always be goofing off during practice (it is *improv,* not ballet), allowing people to have time to socialize before and after practice keeps them focused on the drills at hand.

A great basic format for practices consists of first warming up, then drilling on a particular area or skill set, and finally practicing the form you will be doing in your upcoming shows. We have found that having different practices hone in on different areas of improv keeps your workouts fresh and varied and also allows people time to really think about which aspects of their comedy they need to work to improve. But before we get into the drills that will work out your improv muscles, we have to talk about getting those muscles warmed up. You do not want to pull anything.

All the Best Improv Stretches: Warming Up

Doing great improv comes from freeing your mind of distractions and building strong chemistry within the troupe. Warm-up drills help wake up both your mind and body and get it into the improv mode of giving and accepting offers and building scenes with your troupe. Below are some of our favorite warm-up drills that do just that, but feel free to seek out more resources or invent your own drills that focus on

IGP PRESENTS:
A Note on Constructive Criticism

After the end of each drill, we have found it to be very productive to break down how the drill went and have a mini-discussion. This often takes the form of people speaking up about what they liked and did not like, what worked and what needed to be improved.

When you have discussions, it is important that you feel comfortable talking about specific scenes you saw or what you did (or did not) like in someone else's comedy. If you are not comfortable giving constructive criticism to your troupe members, they will not feel comfortable telling you what you need to work on. If everyone is too scared to talk about specifics, then no one will get better. Honest criticism should be viewed as a sign of respect, not an insult. It says that you believe your fellow improviser is capable and serious about improving.

Also, in discussions, listen to senior members of the troupe. If there are people who have been with your troupe longer than you have and have done more improv, their insights may be the most well-informed. In our discussions, it often will happen that the starry-eyed younger members discuss what they thought worked and what did not while worldly older members talk about theory and how a different approach could have yielded better results.

The main point here is to talk about improv! Get your ideas out there and try your best to work as a troupe to identify strengths and weaknesses (both across the board and personally) so that you can be doing the best improv you can.

these same principles and have the same effects. After all, improv is about making things up!

Pass the Clap

As the group stands in a circle, one person turns to the person next to him or her and maintains eye contact as they both clap once simultaneously. The person who received "the clap" then turns and passes it along to the next person. Once the clap has gone around the circle a few times, start passing it back and forth across the circle. This is not about speed or trying to fake each other out. Keep a constant rhythm and focus, and be ready for the clap to come to you.

Keys to the Drill: Maintain eye contact, pay attention to the rest of the troupe, and pass along the energy of "the clap."

Shake it Out

If the Hokey-Pokey downed a few energy drinks, it might look something like Shake it Out. Improvisers stand in a circle and put each limb into the middle and shake it out one by one (right arm, left arm, right leg, left leg). There are many iterations of this, but you can start the count at sixteen shakes and go once through all four appendages. Then shake each limb out eight times, then four times, then twice, then once. Jump and shout to garnish it off!

Keys to the Drill: Make eye contact to foster group energy, and get your body excited and ready to move!

Zip! Zap! Zop!

An improv classic! Stand in a circle and point (or use a directed clap) to pass the energy across to another player. With each pass of energy you say "zip," "zap," or "zop" in that order. You can increase the speed and try to continue as long as you can without someone saying a word out of order.

Keys to the Drill: Similarly to Pass the Clap, maintain eye contact, pay attention to your troupe, and pass the energy.

Post-Racial Swordsperson (Formerly Called Samurai)

Stand in a circle. One player begins as the post-racial swordsperson. He (or she!) lifts an imaginary sword with a big yell above his (or her!) head. The two players on either side of that person then yell and mime chopping the swordsperson's belly with their swords, and then with the biggest yell of all the swordsperson swings down his (or her!) sword and passes the energy across the circle. The player who catches the energy then becomes the new swordsperson, while people on either side slice him (or her!) in half.

Keys to the Drill: Maintain high energy!

"Yes"

Stand as a group in a circle. One player makes eye contact and points to someone across the circle. The person being pointed at returns the eye contact and says, "Yes!" The first person then walks across the circle to take the place of the second. Meanwhile, the second player now has to point and be accepted by a new person so that he can vacate his spot before the first player gets there. The new person being pointed at says "Yes!" and the second person begins to move. Continue the drill and you should have a constant motion of people accepting each other's offers and crossing the circle.

Keys to the Drill: Listen and wait to move until the person you are pointing at accepts your offer.

Three-Line Scenes

After we warm up, the first drill we start practices with is Three-Line Scenes. This drill helps to build the default of a *two-person scene* where you establish a strong relationship within the *first three lines.* If you can master this drill, improvising in a show should be a snap.

Two scene partners take the stage. The rest of the troupe forms two separate lines. Partner A says a line, Partner B says a line, Partner A says a response. A three-line scene!

Try to establish as much of a relationship and setting as possible in those three lines. Do not leave the audience clueless as to what is going on. When the two partners are done, they head to the back of the *opposite* line from the one they were in before, so everyone can get a chance at initiating a scene. The people at the front of the two lines step forward and start a new scene.

Keys to the Drill: Switch up partners! Do not go with the same person every time.

Areas of Focus

Once warmed up and ready for scene work, you can pick an area of focus for your practice. What follows are a few areas of focus, which include listening and acceptance, strong characters, character status, physicality, and finding a game. Drills accompany each area of focus.

Listening and Acceptance

We have said it before and we will say it again: The key to tight, coherent, and hilarious improvised scenes is *listening* to your scene partner and *accepting* the offers you are given. Failure to listen to your partner creates scenes that do not make sense. If your partner says, "I brought home some fish, honey!" and you, without listening, respond by saying, "Well then, let's go fishing," no one in the audience will be impressed.

When you are performing in front of a live audience of excited fans, their *only* job is to listen to you, while your job is to perform for them and listen to your partner at the same time. Great improvisers can listen almost as well as an audience member can *and* play a character at the same time. Performing improv is much harder than watching it — as it should be!

Listening and acceptance are two separate concepts, but they go hand in hand. Terrific improv scenes feature scene partners building ideas one on top of the other, like bricks in a Great Wall of Improv: very funny, yet impenetrable to Mongolians. When an improviser suggests something that is *not* accepted, a scene can quickly fall apart and suffer from excessive randomness — a bunch of crazy offers pile up like rubble. Thus, listening is key. You have to be able to hear your partner's offers in order to put them into action. What follows are drills that emphasize *listening* and *acceptance*.

Word Association

This drill is a simple warm-up that should not last more than a minute or two, but it emphasizes both listening and building upon your partner's suggestions — accepting. Improvisers stand in a circle and one person starts off by saying a random word. The next person in the circle says a new word that is related to the previous word. This continues, traveling in a circle round and round — a spinning top of related but random suggestions.

This drill emphasizes listening because you must hear and think about the previous word to think about your own. It emphasizes acceptance because you cannot go in a completely new direction. An example of this game would sound like this: "Tree. Branch. Bank. Money. Green. New. Old. Grandmother. Hatred." And so on, as long as there is a relationship, i.e. you hate your grandmother.

You can make this game even more complicated by stipulating that the first letter of each new word be the same as the last letter of the previous word — and related! This makes the challenge of listening and accepting even more difficult. Example: "Gymnastics. Somersault. Tumultuous. Storm. Murdering. Grandmother." That is, if you associate storms with murder. We have already established that you hate your grandmother.

Keys to the Drill: In this drill, there is a tendency to focus on the word of the person *before* the person before you. If the person two before you says "money" and then the person before you says "green," you could still be thinking of "money," and then it comes to you and you say "funds!" But "funds" have nothing to do with "green." Stay in the moment and focus directly on the person before you.

Back-to-Back Drill

Being a good listener means letting what is said really be absorbed. In this drill, you break off into partners and each sit back-to-back. The partners are given a relationship by the rest of the troupe, for example child and babysitter. You then improvise the lines of a scene with your partner (no physicality as you are sitting), while the rest of the group listens.

The only caveat is that your partner must think carefully about what you said before he or she speaks. There can be an indefinite amount of pause before each person says his or her line. The most important aspect of this drill is listening. Each partner must take some time before responding, trying to think of the best, most accepting response possible.

After a few lines are exchanged back and forth, the partners pause and a new set of two improvisers start. In a longer version of this drill, all the groups get to return to their relationship at least once, after some time has passed.

Keys to the Drill: Many people have the tendency to use this drill (and the fact that their partner is forced to pause and listen) to perform a long monologue or to speak too much. The point of this drill is to have normal lines of dialogue, only with extended pauses in between. Try to cut down on the more wordy improvisers in your troupe!

Yes, Yes, Yes

This drill is very simple and focuses entirely on acceptance (and listening, by extension — you have to hear an offer in order to accept it!).

Two performers improvise a scene with a suggestion. The only difference is that one improviser must start each line with "Yes" and then he or she can add anything at all. This improviser is *forced* to accept. The drill cycles through scenes until everyone has had a chance to be a "yes man" (or "yes woman").

Keys to the Drill: Whoever leads this drill must strictly ensure that people say "yes." Some people find it hard to stick to and must be disciplined with a hard ruler and a stern grimace! Additionally, some people tend to cop out by saying lines like, "Yeah ... I don't think I can do that." That is not saying yes. That is saying no in a clever disguise.

Also, the unrestricted partner in the scene, who can say whatever, must be careful not to pose every line as a question — this can be an easy crutch because he or she knows the partner will say "Yes!" automatically, but it should be avoided.

Strong Characters

Pushing yourself to create unique and memorable characters will naturally create equally amazing scenes. When you watch any dramatic performance, it is the characters that stand out, more than the situations they are put into. Some of comedy's greatest heroes became who they were through their characters — think Charlie Chaplin's Tramp or any of the Marx Brothers.

Creating a great character does not require crazy voices or off-the-wall antics. You do not have to have the body of a contortionist or the vocal range of an opera singer to take on different roles. Instead, a great character is a person, perhaps an odd person but a person nonetheless, *grounded* in his or her own world. No matter how outlandish your character is, the character should have real emotions and real hopes and dreams. If a character is grounded, it will be easier to keep that character consistent. If you start a scene as neurotic-but-lovable Larry Wigglemaster, the audience will want you to end your scene as neurotic-but-lovable Larry Wigglemaster.

Strong characters lead to strong scene choices. If you know your character, you will know the decisions they will make. Below are drills to help you step into character.

Character Swap

Start a two-person scene with both performers embodying wildly exaggerated characters that have easy-to-spot mannerisms. After the first three lines, stop the scene and swap out one person for a new person. This new scene partner should fully take on the character that the first scene partner created.

What makes this drill effective is that improvisers can embody characters they never would have otherwise. If there are certain physicalities or personalities that you as an improviser would naturally avoid, this drill forces you to try those out. The more varied your cast of improvisers, the more new kinds of characters you will pick up.

Keys to the Drill: This is not caricature. Even though the initial scene consists of exaggerated characters, the job here is not to create an impersonation. Instead of playing the character over-the-top, make your second version of a character honest.

Character Muse

Again, this is a drill focused on strong two-person scenes. Before the scene starts, the scene partners are both given a common muse from whom they can draw to create a character. For example, the partners can both be told to create a character out of their "worst grade school nemesis" or their "seventh grade math teacher." To make it even more varied, each partner can be given a different muse. "Least favorite aunt" can do a scene with "most awkward acquaintance."

Keys to the Drill: It is important here not to emulate your scene partner. Do not create the same character even if you are both trying to act like your "high school crush." (Or maybe you will discover you had the same high school crush — awkward!) Add variety to the scene by trying to be as different from your partner as possible.

Character Factory

The improviser paces back and forth across the stage, as the rest of the troupe gives him or her instructions as to how to behave. For example, "Walk more slowly," "Bend over more," "Stick out your chest!" When the troupe has decided that the product is complete, the improviser continues to pace, allowing their gait and posture to inform who they are. Once the improviser is comfortable, he or she steps to the front of the stage and introduces himself or herself as the new character.

This should be repeated for a second person, and then the two partners should perform a scene using the characters their troupe created. Like a doctor, the troupe gets to play God with the improvisers, completely altering their gait and the way they carry themselves.

Keys to the Drill: If a group of people tells you to move yourself differently, it can be very hard to keep this new behavior *consistent*. The troupe must take note when improvisers drop traits they have assumed and force them to maintain their new posture or walk.

High or Low: Character Status

Even if it is not on your mind, every relationship you have has a *status* assigned to it. Status, in this case, does not imply wealth or position. It implies the way you behave toward another person. A high-status character can be bossy, domineering, or hostile, even if the character lives in a makeshift hut in a sewer. A low-status character can be awkward, submissive, or fearful, even if that character is an astronaut king who rules over all the land ... and space.

Often, when two improvisers perform together, each can have a tendency to act a certain status. Some improvisers will always be the shouting, warrior chieftain, even if they say they are playing a peasant child. It is therefore very important to vary your status from scene to scene.

Status can manifest itself in any number of ways. It can be how characters speak, how they carry themselves, or how and when they make eye contact. Still, it is not as simple as saying that loud characters have high status. A character can be quiet but *in charge*. Several drills can be used to explore status.

Status Numbers

This drill requires some high-level math. Each scene partner is *secretly* assigned a number from one to five and then must act out a scene with a status of that number. A five is extremely high status and a one is extremely low status.

The two partners perform a scene. Any combination of numbers can make for an interesting scene. Ones can face off against Fours, or Twos can go against other Twos — anything is possible! Each different combination will produce a new result.

If you want to add some fun to the game, have each improviser guess at the end what the other number was. This leads to statements such as "You were definitely a four! *What?* You were a three? No way! I will have to redo all of my calculations!"

Keys to the Drill: Again, the key here is consistency. If you are given a number, stick with it. Do not change your status midway through a scene. Additionally, it can often be fun to assign improvisers numbers that are far from their usual status. If an improviser is typically meek onstage, make him or her a five.

Low to High, High to Low

In this game, each of the two scene partners start off with an opposite status. One player has a very high status and the other has a very low status. A one and a five, so to speak. Then, over the course of the scene, they slowly shift to the other status. The low goes high, the high goes low. This is what Mark Twain was getting at with *The Prince and the Pauper*.

Keys to the Drill: Make sure both partners are subtle in their switch. Improvisers cannot go from shouting at the top of their lungs to begging on their knees all in five seconds. Sudden shifts of emotion are great, but in this drill they are too easy a fallback.

Slaps and Hugs

This drill is similar to the Status Numbers drill, but this time the number you are given dictates how you treat the other person. If you are given a five, you must treat your partner like he or she is the most important person in the world. If you are given a one, your partner is the kind of dirt you would not even put in your mouth for money. The status in your two-person scene is thus affected by how you treat your partner.

Keys to the Drill: Try not to exaggerate. Just because someone is a five does not mean you have to slobber all over that person. Maybe it means you respect them in a calm way. Like prophets and their disciples.

Using Your Body: Physicality

You can improvise almost anywhere. All you need are a couple chairs and some open space. You do not need fancy props or costumes, and that is the beauty of the art. Instead of using props or sets, your actions instead endow your space with details.

It is important to reiterate that physicality allows the audience to imagine where you are and what you are doing. Want to make a phone call? Pull out an imaginary cell phone from your imaginary pocket and go to town. Want to make it rain? Pull out an imaginary umbrella, open it, and now it is raining.

Top Ten Favorite IGP Physicalities You Can Use as a Fallback

pouring a drink
chopping up food
digging a trench
washing a car
taking a shower
painting a wall
cutting down a tree
striking a match
fishing in a boat
applying makeup

Creating a vibrant imaginary space will make your scene work much more interesting. Your audience will not enjoy watching scene after scene take place with you standing around with your partner. They want to see action and that is where you can make it up with your hands.

Pantomime is not the only necessary element of improv. Some people are not that good at using their bodies to tell a story. If that is not your forte, other skills will bolster your improvisational ability. However, it helps to be able to consistently and clearly create a space for your audience to imagine. You should be able to open up an imaginary can of soda with your hands and take a fizzy sip.

The following drills will help you have clear and consistent physicalities.

ABC Room

One by one, each player enters an imaginary room, adding one detail to it with each trip through. For example, the first player could open the door, thus showing the other players whether this is a sliding door, swinging door, or just a bunch of beads hanging from the ceiling. The second player could open the door and wash his or her hands, showing the other players how the sink works. By the end of the drill, the room is a clearly defined space.

As an extension of this drill, the players can then do a set of two-person or group scenes in this space, remembering to keep their actions consistent with the way the room was defined in the drill.

Keys to the Drill: This drill requires incredible focus. By not paying attention, a player can entirely change the way the room is oriented. "Hey, now the bookcase is in the refrigerator! I'm reading eggs!"

Another key is not to add too much. If a player comes into the room, feeds the cat, throws the can opener at the television, and slides back the picture frame to reveal a hidden room, he or she has added too much to the space and will confuse future entrants to the room.

Action Drill

Two players begin by turning their backs to each other. As soon as they cannot see what the other player is doing, they each choose a physicality. One player can wash clothes while the other shelves books. Or one player can knit a scarf while the other digs a ditch.

The players then turn around and begin a scene. The goal in this drill is to let that initial physicality help inform both your character and your scene. Remember, do not lose the physicality you began with as soon as you start talking. Keep doing what you are doing as the scene goes along. If you are knitting a scarf, it is important not to drop your needles. How will you ever finish the scarf that way?

Keys to the Drill: It is important to make sure this drill does not devolve into a discussion of your actions. The dialogue should not be "Wow, you're ice-skating while I'm skinning a tiger! Only in America!" Focus on forming a relationship, and let the comedy flow from there. Meanwhile, maintain consistency with your action and let an interesting scene develop as you reconcile the two actions, moving the story forward.

Don't Talk About It

As they perform a scene, two players take part in a two-person task. For example, they could be washing a car or painting a wall. In this scene, the players *cannot* mention the task as they are doing it. For example, two loggers should be discussing their wives, not the tree they are cutting down.

The players must maintain the physicality throughout the drill. They should also try to add some variety to their actions. Maybe, in addition to painting a wall, they also have to open up a new can of paint.

Keys to the Drill: As the name implies, do not talk about it! This is trickier than you may think. But the entire point of this drill is to not talk about what you are doing. Of course, the very existence of the rule makes it harder to follow. Seize the challenge — this is your moment!

Finding a Game: Pattern

Notice that none of the drills mentioned have told you how to practice being funny. That is like asking a politician to practice being charming or asking a beautiful person to practice being beautiful. You can hone associated skills like physicality or character, but it is a tall order to practice "being funny."

These next few drills ask you to do just that. Many of the most successful improv scenes have a pattern. In the previous chapter we described it as the *game* of the scene. It can be hard to practice finding the game, but it is your job as an improviser (both on the sidelines and in the scene) to notice these patterns and exploit them for laughs. Creating a game in a scene can be as simple as noticing what is funny and then attempting to repeat it. These drills will help you to mine the patterns of scenes for their humor.

Fast Forward Five Days

Often, scenes are lost in exposition, as characters slowly discover who they are and what they are doing. For an audience, this can be very boring to watch. Scene partners will benefit if they can jog past the exposition and get straight to the meat. In this drill, two scene partners improvise a regular scene. After the first line that elicits a laugh, someone offstage yells "Fast forward!" The scene partners continue the scene five days later or five years or five hours — go ahead and experiment with different types of time travel.

Moving forward in time allows the players to move past the exposition, and they can then mine the initial humor of the scene for more laughs. For example, let's imagine an initial scene where a husband wants to leave his wife after having been married for only a couple hours. The humor comes from the fact that the husband wants to end something he just started. Now fast forward five days, what patterns can we find? Perhaps the husband has just quit a job he started the day before, or maybe the wife wants to return a dog they just picked up from the pound that morning. By moving the scene forward in time, patterns can be easier to tease out.

Keys to the Drill: It can be easy to make the humor of the scene merely that two people are still doing the same thing they did five days ago. The audience will laugh and say, "Wow, they are still fighting!" and then quickly become very bored. Avoid this type of easy joke.

Pattern Tag

This drill requires four people: two scene partners and two crafty, manipulative people on the sidelines. The two people onstage perform an improvised scene, while the two people on the sidelines wait until a pattern emerges, typically the first big laugh.

When the first laugh comes, the two people offstage tag out the improvisers onstage and do a brand new scene, amplifying the pattern that made them edit the scene. They are new characters in a new situation, using the humor from the previous scene to inspire their new scene. For example, if the first scene is about two boxers who are too courteous to punch each other, the second scene could be about two cannibals too courteous to eat each other.

Keys to the Drill: This drill requires two people on the sidelines who can easily identify when something is funny and what the pattern is behind it. If this proves to be too tricky, another method can be to interrupt the two players onstage, ask them why what they are doing is funny, and then have them continue to amplify that without tagging them out. (See the next drill.)

Directed Scenes

This drill requires two scene partners and an all-powerful prophet-like character on the sidelines who can tell them what to do. If there is someone you know who has the experience or insight to be a director on the sidelines, seize the opportunity to be told how to improvise. In directed scenes, the director interrupts the improvisers with tips, helping them to focus on patterns or heightening the emotion or stakes of the scene.

Are directed scenes still improvised? Here is a clear, concise answer: in a way they are and in a way they are not. You can do what you want, with the safety net of someone who is willing to tell you that it is not working.

Keys to the Drill: There is a delicate balance between interrupting the right amount and meddling too much. If a scene has to stop every fifteen seconds, it is being *over*-directed and under-improvised.

These pattern drills are some of the hardest in this chapter, and if you can master these, you are set to have very successful practice sessions, as you are grasping what improv scenes are all about.

Congratulations, your life is finally coming together. You have meaning now.

The Most Important Drill: Have Fun

To return to sports metaphors: We have all seen those movies where a team of lovable losers gets together and beats the favored (and unlikeable) team. You might have noticed that most of their training montage is them having fun and bonding. Be those lovable losers. Nothing about improv should be stressful. Save that for *every other aspect* of your life. Let improv be your safe space.

Along those lines, when you practice improv, you should be having fun. In some ways, practices can be more fun than performing improv for an audience. Low expectations make the funniest lines shine through. If you are not having fun while practicing improv as a group, talk about it with your fellow improvisers. Figure out some drills that work for you, and do not stick with drills that do not. None of the drills in this chapter are essential to good improv — most of them have evolved as IGP tried them out. (Hint: you will hate 10 percent of the drills in this chapter.)

Encourage your fellow improvisers to make up their own drills. One of IGP's favorite drills is called "Landmine Monster," and it is completely quirky and homegrown. If someone yells "monster," the scene partners have to amplify their emotions. If someone yells "landmine," the scene partners have to change course and explore a different topic. That is it. There is no greater meaning. But it is something we came up with during practice one day while we were just having fun.

Try collaborating with other troupes to learn new drills or techniques for having exceptional practices. If you can afford it, have a workshop with a professional to get new takes on improv drills and focus on new skills. Steal the best of what they tell you and incorporate it into your practices. Remember, there is no copyright on an improv drill.

At least, we really, really hope not. We could be in some legal hot water that needs to be resolved. But until then, keep practicing.

Chapter Five
SHORT-FORM OR LONG-FORM: THE ETERNAL DEBATE

"IT'S SHORT-FORM. VERY SHORT."

Eight years ago, the Immediate Gratification Players almost separated in an improv civil war. Some members had begun meeting in secret to practice a new form of improv — long-form. While half of IGP wanted the troupe to keep performing short-form, the others had newer ideas ...

Once you are comfortable with the idea of doing improv, one of the most important decisions you will need to make is what kind of improv you want to do. No matter how funny your troupe might be, you will need some kind of organizational structure to your performances. Otherwise, you will just be telling a stream of disconnected jokes for thirty minutes, which is difficult to do. (Ask any stand-up comedian.)

Broadly speaking, there are two basic forms of improv: short-form and long-form. In short-form, your troupe performs a variety of different games, each with its own unique, unrelated rules and structure. In long-form, you work from a single suggestion and develop a loosely linked series of scenes that emphasize characters and relationships. There are advantages and disadvantages to both, but whichever form you choose will directly impact what sort of jokes you tell, what types of drills you focus on, and, ultimately, what kind of troupe your little band of funny people becomes.

The Immediate Gratification Players are a long-form improv troupe, but we sometimes perform short-form. Thus, we have tasted both types of improv cuisine. We will start by taking a look at what makes each form distinctive, and then we can take a look at which form is right for you.

Short-Form Improv: It's Game(s) Time!

Short-form improv has one outstanding advantage: it is well-known even to people who are otherwise unfamiliar with improvisational comedy. The fame of the format is largely to the credit of one very popular, very long-running show. At this point, it is not just a cliché to mention the TV show *Whose Line Is It Anyway?*; it is practically required by law.

The show spotlighted short-form improv for an astounding eighteen seasons and 363 episodes in both its British and American versions, and it is still what most people first think about when improv is mentioned. Even though the show went off television almost a decade ago and even though the improv IGP does is not remotely similar to what was on *Whose Line?*, it remains our go-to explanation when we explain what we do to those who do not know a whole lot about improv.

The format of *Whose Line?* was simple: four improvisers competed for arbitrary "points" by participating in various improv games. The games could feature any combination and any number of the improvisers, from the occasional monologue to two-person scenes to group games. The objective and structure of each game often differed greatly.

Sometimes one improviser had to guess what was going on in a scene based on clues from his fellow performers, sometimes improvisers were tasked with recreating a particular kind of TV show, like a telethon or newscast, and sometimes they had to come up with the best one-liners based on a given prop or situation.

The structure of *Whose Line?* speaks to a basic point about short-form improv: generally speaking, any given scene has an objective that the performers are ostensibly working toward, and often that objective is not simply to be funny. The humor is a by-product of trying to complete the primary goal.

There are two reasons short-form is made up of a bunch of disconnected scenes. The boring, practical reason is because each scene has its own rules and limitations; thus, you need to reset after each scene so that the host can explain the next one's structure. The fun, theoretical reason behind all this is that every new scene is a new opportunity to get suggestions from the audience. According to a peer-reviewed scientific study that we just made up, nothing fires up a crowd more than a chance to yell out suggestions, and short-form gives them plenty of opportunities.

Things That Get Improv Audiences Fired Up

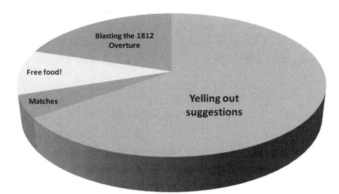

Blasting the 1812 Overture

Free food!

Matches

Yelling out suggestions

Source: The Holy Fish Comedy Institute

Like we mentioned earlier, the members of IGP who performed improv in high school did short-form. In fact, we can confidently estimate that 95 percent of all high school improv troupes do short-form. (We got that statistic from the same place we got our audience participation study.)

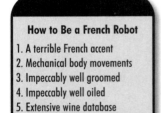

How to Be a French Robot
1. A terrible French accent
2. Mechanical body movements
3. Impeccably well groomed
4. Impeccably well oiled
5. Extensive wine database

There are a number of reasons for this. Perhaps the most fundamental one is that it is a lot easier to grasp the point of short-form games for audiences and performers alike. High school audiences often want to see their peers playing games and making fools of themselves, not necessarily finding humor in character and relationship. And if you are just starting out as an improviser, which task sounds clearer: To act like a French robot in a game of "Party Quirks," or to just, well ... create something funny? Sure, people get into improv because they feel they are funny enough to entertain people, but what does "be funny" mean when it comes time to put on a show? "French robot" is a concrete crowd-pleaser, if more than a little bizarre.

Short-form is great because its very structure is designed to create laughs. Consider the Alphabet Game, where you and your partner need to start each sentence with each successive letter of the alphabet.

(So if the first letter is "H," the first three sentences might be "*Hey* there," "*I* did not expect to see you here," and "*Just* passing through.") The audience is already entertained when you can come up with a word starting with "X" or "Z" on command, whether or not you also turn the subsequent sentences into jokes.

Going back to our example of Pierre-X37, the French robot, there are a lot of ways in which you trying to make your scene partner understand that you are a French robot could be funny. Only one of them is that your performance is objectively hilarious. The host of the party might prove completely incapable of deducing that you are a robot, French or otherwise, leading to a series of increasingly preposterous, desperate guesses. It might turn out that you are utterly incapable of doing a French accent, especially when also asked to sound like a robot. Your attempts might well prove comically terrible.

Is any of that "good" improv in the sense of sticking to the fundamentals? No, not really, but it can be a great show. There is an excellent chance that the audience will find it hilarious as long as everyone involved is obviously trying their best. Part of improv's inherent appeal is that most people find it so impossibly difficult to do – or even to imagine doing. The moment when audiences truly realize, "My God! They are making it up!" is sometimes the most important part of the show, as that is when they have been won over.

As such, audiences tend to grade scenes in short-form improv on a pretty forgiving curve, and part of that is the fact that the structure of the games can often seem so ridiculous. After all, why *should* you be able to do a perfect impersonation of a French robot? The fact that you *chose* to play a game that would ask you to do that is irrelevant. Audiences enjoy failure in improv almost as much as they enjoy success. This can be a reassuring position to be in when you are just starting out as an improv troupe.

I Know Some Good Games We Can Play ...

While we are discussing the theory of short-form improv, it is probably helpful to mention a few of the games you can choose to perform. There are thousands of possibilities, but here are a few of the more famous ones:

1. Party Quirks – Four performers. One performer, the host, is sent out of the theatre so he or she cannot hear the audience's suggestions. The other three are given weird quirks. These might include "talk show host," "lonely grizzly bear," or "man time

traveling through his own life," just to name three examples IGP would love to hear someone in the audience yell. The host then has to guess what roles the three performers have been given based on their performances.

2. Shoulda Said — Two performers plus a referee. This is basically a regular scene, but the referee can decide when a line could be funnier and command them to change it by yelling "Shoulda Said!" Also known as "Change It," "Rewrite," "Ding," and about a dozen other aliases.

3. World's Worst — An entire improv troupe. Using a bunch of suggestions from the audience, the improvisers have to come up with anything from "world's worst car salesman" to "world's worst Mother's Day gift." This game is pretty heavy on the one-liners, as many of the lines are simply said and not performed.

4. Questions Only — Four performers. Two improvisers start a scene where both can only ask questions. If one of them fails to ask a question, repeats a question, or just generally cracks up, that performer leaves and is replaced by one of the two others waiting in the wings.

5. Two-Line Vocab — Three performers. Two of the improvisers only have two lines of dialogue each: a statement and a question. Their job is to find as many different ways to give meaning to the same set of words through intonation, while the performer in the middle has the rather more difficult task of making the scene hang together.

6. Make Up Your Own Game — Any number of performers. The beauty of short-form is that the number of games are infinite. Design your own structure and you can go from there. Tip: Make it easy to explain to an audience!

Long-Form Improv: All in the Relationships

Long-form improv is what most professional theatres perform, as well as many college improv troupes. It is arguably the more subtle and technically demanding of the two forms. (But, hey, we are a little biased, are we not?) In its simplest incarnation, known as a "Montage," the improv troupe takes a single one-word suggestion, and then the improvisers are completely on their own. For the next twenty to forty minutes, there is no stopping, no restarting, no trying a new game if the current one is no longer working. It is just the improvisers, the suggestion, and whatever scenes and relationships they can come up with. That can be a pretty daunting prospect.

The key to successful long-form improv is complete commitment to the fundamentals of good improvisational comedy. In short-form, there are a lot of games where these concepts take a backseat to the stated rules. It can be hard to really *build a strong relationship* with your scene partner or *create a vivid character* when your first objective is to help her deduce your party quirk. And it can be pretty hard to *not put your scene partner on the spot* and force him to be funny when playing something like *The Dating Game,* which is all about asking open-ended questions. Indeed, it is by definition impossible to *avoid asking questions* in the game Questions Only, for reasons that are hopefully self-explanatory. As explained earlier, the trade-off in sacrificing your better improv instincts is that the audience tends to be more forgiving when you mess up. In a long-form, you are more clearly relying on the fundamentals you have drilled into your head, but the margin for error is a lot smaller.

This is because the objective of long-form is really quite straightforward. Like we suggested earlier, the scenes must be funny on their own. If you are not being funny, there is not much an audience can enjoy at an *improvised comedy* show. Failure in a silly game like Party Quirks can be endearing and get laughs. When you fail while doing long-form, it is just sort of, well, *unfunny.*

But fear not! There might be less of a comedic safety net in long-form, but there are still a few things to fall back on. Most basically, there is the relationship between the characters in a scene. In a short-form game, it often does not matter all that much what the characters' specific connection is. The game of Change It might be *better* if the two characters had a clear, well-realized relationship, but the scene can still be funny if it is just a couple of random dudes so long as the new and improved lines are quick and consistently amusing. The focus there is not on the relationship; it is on following the rules of the game by changing lines.

In a long-form performance, however, it is crucial that the performers flesh out their relationship in any given scene and make it vivid. Let's look at an example. Two people are in a scene. What is their connection? Maybe they are a mother and son. That is a solid choice — it is a fairly universal relationship that most people can relate to one way or another.

But how do they feel about each other? What do they want from each other? How old are they? Who has the power in the relationship? These are the kind of questions the performers in any given long-form scene should be able to answer, or at least should be thinking about.

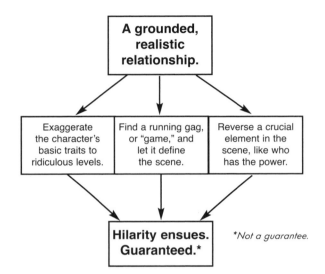

IGP PRESENTS:
Gauging Audience Reaction

One of the most fascinating experiences in improv is the different set of reactions you tend to receive when you do short-form or long-form. Based on our experience having performed both forms, there is a clear distinction in what audience members pick up on during a show.

After a short-form show, people tend to say how funny you were or how hilarious a particular line was. In a long-form show, the reaction is different. People tend to focus more on how funny the characters you played were or how good certain scenes were. We leave you to draw your own conclusion, but it goes without saying that that is incredibly profound and significant.

Neither performer knows any of this before the scene starts — indeed, they should not even know their relationship until they hit the stage — but each can make decisions about their relationship and then offer that to their scene partner.

Maybe the son is now an adult, and he has become distant from his mother over the years. Perhaps, despite this, the mother still supports her son financially, and her otherwise proud son has come home to ask for more money. And maybe, even though the mother controls the purse strings, she loves her son too much to ever say no.

Now, that might not sound all that funny. In fact, that scenario might sound more like the stuff of Russian drama, or at the very least Norwegian. (Something Scandinavian, at any rate. The point is it's not a comedy.) But it is all in how you play the scene. Perhaps the mother is just so completely oblivious to her son's manipulation that the audience cannot help but laugh. The performers might be able to latch onto the idea of the mother giving things to her son and turn it into a running gag (or, if you are feeling pretentious, a motif), where the mother keeps giving her son increasingly absurd items, starting small with something like a cup of tea and finishing with his own small country.

In improv parlance, this is called (can you guess it by now?) a *game,* and it is one of the most consistent ways to find humor in a long-form scene. Basically, that is the general aim of long-form scenes: to take something very real and grounded, like a son who needs financial help from his mother, and turn it into something comically absurd. If you do it right, the laughs will follow.

The takeaway message is that, although there are not really any set rules in long-form, the best scenes are those in which the performers can create their own rich structure. The two performers in our example scene did not start with any set quirks they had to guess or specific questions they had to ask. Rather, they established a basic relationship of mother and son and then colored it in with a lot of specific details, which they were then able to twist and invert for comedic purposes. The best part is, when a long-form troupe is really grooving, it does not even particularly matter if the scene is all that funny. Sometimes, the relationship itself can be more than compelling enough to hold the audience's attention.

So Which One Is Right for You?

Honestly, there is no single right answer to the question of which form is best. You probably are going to want to experiment with both and see what feels right. Maybe your group is naturally strong at building scenes and creating characters. That might suggest long-form is for you. Perhaps one of your strengths is interacting with the audience and getting them jumping and shouting out crazy suggestions. In that case, short-form may be better for you. Trial and error is your friend here. Go hang out with it.

But still, there are some general recommendations we can make. If your newly-formed troupe is pretty much made up of beginners to improv, then short-form is probably the way to go. It has a gentler learning curve, your group is more likely to have some familiarity with it, and it is a lot easier to get a newly-created short-form troupe ready for its first performance than its long-form counterpart. If your main goal is to get out there and make people laugh as quickly as possible, then short-form is the better bet.

If, on the other hand, you are really looking to hone your improv skills and challenge yourself, then you might want to seriously consider long-form. It is definitely a more challenging endeavor, particularly for those just starting out, but the rewards can be tremendous. We can put it like this: because of the bigger safety net that all the rules in short-form provide, a bad short-form will never be as terrible as a bad long-form. When long-form shows bomb, they really bomb. Still, there is nothing that quite compares to a well-executed long-form show, with the troupe firing on all cylinders and building strong relationships quickly and vividly. As good as short-form can be, it has trouble comparing with long-form at its absolute best.

We subtitled this chapter "The Eternal Debate" in reference to whether troupes should do short-form or long-form, and we stand by that. (We are fairly sure this question is what the Council of Nicaea was about. Also, the Hundred Years War.)

But we will also completely contradict ourselves and point out that lots of troupes happily do both with great success. After all, if the guiding principle of improv is to say yes, then how can you say no when both forms have so much to offer? The only question now is how to get the most out of each form. Luckily, we have answers to that, too.

IGP PRESENTS:
Get Rich the Improvised Way (Maybe)!

It has been brought to our attention that some people out there might not feel that spending all of your waking hours reading, rereading, and memorizing this book, which we just naturally assume you are doing, is a great idea. After all, it is not like improv is going to help you become financially independent, right? Wrong!

There is plenty of money to be made in improv both right now and in the future, and we will tell you which form you should focus on for either goal. That is right, we wrote this sidebar so that you can show it to your parents or significant other and prove to them that this is a useful book that will help set you up for financial independence in the future. They will like that. You are welcome.

If you want to be a professional improviser, you probably will want to commit to long-form. It is the dominant form for pretty much every major professional improv organization, and it has the added bonus of focusing on and sharpening the improv fundamentals that you will need to master if you want to go pro.

However, if you are looking to get paying gigs in the here and now, then short-form is the way to go. Without question. Whenever IGP manages to luck into paid shows (we have performed for such diverse groups as a principals' convention and a meeting of geriatric care professionals, and you can too!) we always do short-form. In these situations, when we are performing as a bit of light entertainment at the start of their meeting, groups tend to like something that is familiar, not too long, and high on audience participation. Short-form is perfect for that.

Chapter Six
IT'S SHOWTIME:
DEVELOPING A FORMAT

Improv has an incredible number of games and formats. The Harold. The Montage. Shoulda Said. Party Quirks. VHS. DVD. Poodle. Golden Retriever.

These formats are not set in stone, either. You have the power to make brand new ones yourself. How else would someone have thought up the 24-Hour Show, in which troupes improvise for an entire day?

Any improv format is merely a method intended to create spontaneity and excite the audience. So try a few out and get good at one of them. Then, when you can, mix and match to create something new ...

So you have honed your skills and decided to either do long-form or short-form — now it is time to develop a format. Your format is the structure of your show; it is how you will organize your short-form games or the framework you will use to perform your long-form.

Before we present and analyze potential formats that your troupe might want to use, we must first note that it is impossible to give an exhaustive list of all possible improv formats. Improv can look fifty different ways and is constantly evolving. (That is the theory, anyway.)

While we will present plenty of formats here, we encourage you to utilize other resources, namely the Internet, to find out about other short-form games and long-form structures. Also, once you feel comfortable, do not hesitate to create your own.

The comedic and improvisational instincts you have been developing in practice mean nothing if you do not have a way to present them. For the remainder of the chapter, we will advise you on how to structure a short-form show and also present to you a series of long-form formats.

You need a way to put your talents on full display. A peacock can have beautiful feathers, but potential mates will never know if he does not show them off. Here are some suggestions for how to fan out your tail!

A Short-Form Show: Putting Games Together

It should not come as much of a surprise that the format for a short-form show is just the stringing together of a few short-form games. What is nice about this is that once you know which games you are performing, you are ready for a show. However, there are many small things you can do in how you organize and execute your show that can make a big difference in how your audience enjoys it.

First and foremost is energy. It is important that both the performers *and the audience* are energized. Before you begin your show, make sure to warm up your audience. Have them practice yelling out suggestions, do some vocal exercises, get them involved, and promise them monetary rewards. You would not believe how much better a show can be once the audience is warmed up, primed to laugh, and looking forward to a six-figure cash payout. (Tip: audiences *hate* IOUs.)

Sample Audience Warm-Ups
1. Yell out emotions (for example, surprised, concerned, ecstatic) and have the audience respond with corresponding noises and facial expressions.
2. Get a name from someone in the audience (John) and have a few improvisers (A and B) go back and forth performing a rap where the audience needs to guess and yell out the last word of the rhyme.

A: I met this guy, his name was John, I did chores for him, like mow his ... lawn.

B: I met this guy, his name was John, he would always play his guitar and sing a ... song.

A: I met this guy, his name was John, half-goat, half-man, that's right, he's a ... faun.

You play until either the improviser or audience messes up.

Getting an audience prepared to laugh and to enjoy a show begins with keeping them energized and engaged. And while it begins with your opening, the energy needs to be maintained throughout. Short-form games are designed to be fast-paced and joke-heavy, so the energy will take care of itself during these parts of the show. The part of the show where energy can dip is between games. With that in mind, when introducing new games and describing how they are played, make sure to be dynamic yet concise. Minimize the downtime between games and make sure the audience stays engaged.

Another important thing to do when organizing your short-form show is to *vary it up*. This can take the form of game length, type of game, or type of suggestion required for the game. In making your set list before the show, you should consider these factors and make sure there is variation between your games. Some games tend to run long, others are short. Some games involve everyone, some involve just a few. Some games emphasize characters, others are more scene-based. These should all be factored into organizing your show so the audience feels it is always seeing something new.

To help you with this, we have included a short list of categorized games. The more games you learn, the more you practice them, and the more you perform them, the better you will be at organizing them in a manner that best engages the audience. Below, a list of short-form improv games by type.

Entire Troupe Games

1. *Tag-Team Monologue:* Everyone faces the audience and you get a suggestion for an object. One member then steps forward and begins a monologue inspired by the suggestion. He continues to monologue until someone else steps forward, taps him out, and continues the monologue picking up on the last word or syllable said.

2. *Freeze:* This is a classic improv game where two improvisers do a scene until someone offstage yells, "Freeze." At this point, both improvisers freeze, the person who stopped them comes on, taps out one of the performers, assumes his or her position, and then starts a new scene inspired by the physicality he or she has assumed.

3. *World's Worst:* See Chapter Five.

Character Games

1. *Dating Game:* Four performers. The bachelor(ette) leaves the room and the audience assigns characters or quirks to the three potential dates, in a similar fashion to Party Quirks. The bachelor(ette) then returns and must figure out what quirks each date has through a series of questions.

2. *Good, Bad, Worst Advice:* Four performers. The audience provides the topic for a talk show, for example, marital problems, animal husbandry, or interior decorating. The talk show host welcomes his three experts, who all introduce themselves and establish their characters. One gives good advice, one gives bad advice, and one gives the worst advice. The host then fields questions from the audience on the subject that the "experts" then answer.

3. *Party Quirks:* See Chapter Five.

Scene Games

1. *Pocket Lines:* Two or three performers. Before the show, audience members write down lines on pieces of paper. When you play the game, collect the lines and give each performer a few to put in his or her pocket. Do not peek! During the course of the scene, improvisers pull the lines out of their pocket, deliver the lines, and make sure to justify them.

2. *One-Word Exit:* Three performers. The audience gives each performer a word and then a non-geographical setting for the scene. For example, an office, a boat, or, even better, an office-boat. Whenever a performer says someone's word, he must find an excuse to leave the scene if he is onstage or return to the scene if he is offstage.

3. *Shoulda Said:* See Chapter Five.

Putting Games Together for a Show

Putting a bunch of these games together to form a show is a delicate art. You want to start big, maintain the energy throughout, and end with a bang. The best way to demonstrate this is by example. Let's put these tips into action and present a sample short-form improv show.

Game #1: Tag-Team Monologue

This is a good game to start a show. It involves all the members of the troupe and is relatively quick.

Sample Tag-Team Monologue

The audience gives the word "hamburger." The monologue begins as a teenage door-to-door salesman tries to sell hamburgers to people in his neighborhood. Despite his best efforts, he continually gets rejected. Troupe members keep tagging in and trying to convince the potential buyers why they should buy his hamburger. Eventually, the boy goes to his own house where he unsuccessfully pleads with his parents.

Game #2: Shoulda Said

During the introduction to the show and Tag-Team Monologue, everyone has had a chance to be onstage. Now, we ease into the show a little more with everyone leaving except the two performers and the "referee" in this game. With this game, embrace the ridiculousness that tends to rise from having to come up with new lines over and over again.

Game #3: Good, Bad, Worst Advice

This game nicely contrasts with its predecessor, as it requires a lot of audience input and is highly character-based, two things that Shoulda Said does not have.

Sample Good, Bad, Worst Advice

The audience suggests a talk show about easy-to-make meals. The first expert chooses to be a TV cooking personality and gives good advice throughout. The humor comes from an accurate yet exaggerated imitation of the gimmicks used on these cooking programs. The second expert chooses to be a popular and attractive high school quarterback who does his best to answer the audience's questions but often resorts to using unhelpful sports analogies. The final expert is the host's grandfather who forgot his hearing aid at home and continually mishears the questions, giving answers to things that were not actually asked.

Game #4: Pocket Lines

This is an easy game, as most of the humor is in the ridiculous lines sitting in your pocket waiting to be delivered. Make sure to set yourself up each time you use one of the lines and make sure to justify what you say in terms of what is going on in the scene. Depending on your audience, it might be a good idea to have another troupe member screen the lines before playing. Also, be sure to collect the papers from the audience a few games before Pocket Lines so you do not have a break in the action between this game and the previous one.

Game #5: Party Quirks

This is a return to the character-based games. When you play, instead of just having the host interact with the guests, it is helpful for the guests to interact with each other too, as they have the knowledge to be able to give clues about each other's and their own identities. Also, improvisers not in the game can show up to the party, give a hint about a guest, and then leave.

Game #6: One-Word Exit

This is a fast-paced game that nicely contrasts with the sometimes stagnant and talk-heavy Party Quirks. Remember, you have control over making people leave and enter. Utilize that for comedic effect. Make yourself leave sometimes; make someone enter and leave quickly. And unless you want to end the game, make sure not everyone is sent offstage at once.

Game #7: Freeze

We started with a group game and we end with a group game. This is a nice way to end the show as everyone is involved, you get to do many different scenes, and you have complete control over when to end it. For these reasons, Freeze is actually a fairly common way to end a short-form show.

And there you go! A nice forty-minute short-form improv show that successfully organized its games to maximize the enjoyment of the audience (and hopefully maintained a good energy throughout). The beauty of short-form shows is the simplicity — they are just one game after another. Keep playing the games and playing around with how best to structure them in relation to one another and your shows will be huge successes.

IGP PRESENTS:
Explaining a Short-Form Game

The Good. *Alright, so the next game we're going to play is called Party. Megan here is hosting, you guessed it, a party! Now Megan, would you please leave the room? What she doesn't know is that her three guests, Mark, Michelle, and Mike, all are a little ... odd. Can I have some suggestions of odd characters for the three of them? Wonderful. Mark is an escaped panda, Michelle is an assassin, and Mike is a pool boy. Let's get Megan back in here and begin!*

The Bad. *OK. So now we're going to play another game. This game will have four people. Can I get four people? OK, good. It is going to be about a party and about guessing who people are. But it won't be so simple because they are going to be weird people. Megan will be the one guessing. The other three will be the ones acting out characters. I need three characters.*

The Ugly. *I told the barber half bowl cut and half rattail.*

A Long-Form Show: Choose Your Own Adventure

We already know that short-form improv shows divide themselves into games and long-form improv shows divide themselves into scenes. However, unlike with short-form, there exist specific formats for performing and presenting long-form improv scenes. Some of these, like the Harold, have become widely known and are thought of as traditional formats. Others, like IGP's Dinner Party Show, are more experimental. If you plan on performing long-form comedy, it is important to be familiar with these forms and to choose the ones that work best for your troupe.

The Traditional Formats

The Montage is a series of scenes that explore a one-word audience suggestion. The scenes can be completely unrelated to one another, although it is often rewarding for the audience if you incorporate recurring themes and sometimes revisit certain characters.

The first few scenes should really explore the suggestion and its many possible meanings and uses. For example, a show based on the word *train* might have opening scenes about two strangers sharing a room in an overnight train, another scene about a coach training an athlete before the big game, and another scene between a teacher and a parent about how the parent's child is *getting off track* in his studies.

Later in the show, scenes from the beginning can be revisited, characters can be brought back in new situations, and themes can be fleshed out. The strength of these later scenes depends on how well you explored the word at the beginning and created material to inspire future scenes. Remember, the suggestion should be your friend. Let it help you at the start to come up with scenes, but do not let it restrict you later on when you feel like there is no new way to interpret the word. (Train can only mean so many things.) If and when that happens, it is a sign to move away from the word you were given and explore the material and ideas introduced and developed in the scenes you have done already.

The Harold is a famous long-form format developed by Del Close and Charna Halpern. The show is broken into three parts, each with a group game and three scenes. To begin, the audience provides a one-word suggestion that the ensemble of improvisers then explores in a group game. This often takes the form of many small conversations, a word association, monologues, or a physical and verbal exploration of the word. During the game, the ensemble should move away from the literal meaning of the suggested word and find deeper meaning and alternative interpretations.

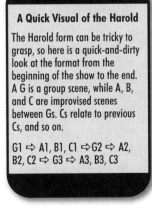

A Quick Visual of the Harold

The Harold form can be tricky to grasp, so here is a quick-and-dirty look at the format from the beginning of the show to the end. A G is a group scene, while A, B, and C are improvised scenes between Gs. Cs relate to previous Cs, and so on.

G1 ⇨ A1, B1, C1 ⇨ G2 ⇨ A2, B2, C2 ⇨ G3 ⇨ A3, B3, C3

Then the first round of scenes begins. Three unrelated two-person scenes take place, inspired by the opening game. This inspiration can inform the setting, certain themes or lines, or perhaps specific objects. These scenes are important for establishing characters and relationships, as the same characters and stories will be revisited during the next two rounds of scenes.

After the first round of scenes, many members of the troupe play a group game unrelated to the scenes that have been performed thus far. Often, however, the group game has some connection to what was brought up during the opening of the show. There are many different forms this group game can take. It can be the telling and acting out of a story, a made up commercial, or a game of freeze-tag, just to name a few.

After the game, a second round of scenes begins. These scenes heighten the action from the first round, often with some lapse in time having occurred. For example, if the first scene of the first round showed two students stealing exam answers from their teacher's desk, the first scene of the second round may be the same two people, now twenty years later, breaking into a bank, or perhaps they are still in jail after having gotten caught cheating on the test. Either way, the scenes should move the story forward the second time around and heighten the conflict.

Once all three scenes have been revisited, there is yet another group game and then the final round of scenes. Here, the structure breaks down a little. The themes, storylines, characters, and games that have been developed throughout the show come together. This time, instead of seeing three separate scenes, it is more likely that the scenes will overlap to a degree and coalesce, as the most interesting and funny aspects of the show return.

As with most formats, there is no definitive way the show should be structured. Some performances of the Harold, for example, ignore the second and third group games, while others include a final group game after the third round of scenes.

The Armando Diaz is a show based around a series of monologues. One improviser takes from the audience a one-word suggestion and begins a monologue (three to five minutes) about a real event in his or her life based on the word. This monologue does not have to be explicitly funny, though it is often somewhat humorous. The rest of the improvisers then perform a series of scenes, similar to the Montage, based on the content of the monologue. It is not an exact acting out of the monologue. Rather, it is an interpretation or an exploration of it. For example, during a monologue based on the word *sibling,* the improviser may say, "Growing up as the youngest of nine kids was tough because everything I got was a hand-me-down." From just this one line, the improvisers might do a scene where a couple makes a pact to have nine children, not for love, but so they can be on a reality television show and another scene in which one guy complains that all the girls he dates are "hand-me-downs," as they have already dated his older brothers. A three- to five-minute monologue provides many things to interpret and develop, so listen carefully.

After fifteen minutes or so of scenes, the improviser performing the monologue returns to give another, this one about something that came up during one of the scenes. The improvisers then return and do scenes based on the second monologue. These scenes can also include storylines, characters, and themes that were introduced in the first round of scenes. After another fifteen minutes, the improviser returns a final time for a closing monologue based on something brought up in the second round of scenes.

Experimental Formats

You need not feel bound to traditional formats. When possible, you can try making up a brand new format that works for you. Here are a few we have made up over the years.

The Dinner Party Show is a signature IGP format that we perform once yearly. Audience members are treated to a dinner where the improvisers sit and eat with them. Once everyone has been served, the show's host gets from the audience an occasion for the dinner party, an appropriate character suggestion for the evening's special guest, a character for the host, and then characters for the other improvisers. The improvisers take turns briefly toasting the special guest, allowing themselves to establish their character and relationship to others, and to hint at potential upcoming action.

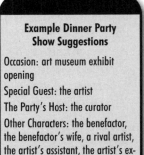

Example Dinner Party Show Suggestions

Occasion: art museum exhibit opening

Special Guest: the artist

The Party's Host: the curator

Other Characters: the benefactor, the benefactor's wife, a rival artist, the artist's assistant, the artist's ex-wife, and the artist's estranged son

After the toasts, improvisers return to their seats with the audience and scenes begin. While eating, the audience watches as the improvisers move around the room interacting with one another in character. During these scenes, typically involving two people, relationships are fleshed out and story lines are developed. Over the course of thirty minutes, the story escalates until it reaches a climax and eventually a conclusion.

Throughout the show, it is paramount that you listen carefully, regardless of whether or not you are in the scene. You need to know what is going on so your scenes add to the central conflict that others have established. Additionally, be aware that your character might not be centrally featured or highly important to the plot. If you are a peripheral character, trust the central characters to utilize you when the plot demands it, and make the most of those opportunities. Do not force yourself into the story!

The Radio Show is performed entirely in the dark. The improvisation is done entirely with your voices, and you can remain seated all throughout the show. (After all, no one will see you, though they will feel your dominating presence.)

One way to perform this show requires an improviser to take on the role of a narrator, who plays an instrumental role in the show and whose ego will grow exponentially. He or she gets from the audience character suggestions for four to six performers, a short list of non-geographical locations, and a few fictional products to be advertised during the show. The lights then go down, the characters introduce themselves, and the show begins.

In the playing of this format, the narrator controls the action by setting up scenes ("We find the ten-year-old detective and the lion tamer at the scene of the crime ... ") that the improvisers then explore. The narrator will transition between scenes when he or she sees fit ("Meanwhile, across town, the poacher takes confession with the priest ... "). He or she will also interrupt the action occasionally for a commercial break during which a few improvisers will advertise one of the suggested products. Eventually the show reaches its climax and conclusion, which can be cued by the narrator ("We now return to the program and its thrilling conclusion where ... ").

Much of the show's success relies on the narrator getting suggestions, pacing the show, setting up scenes, and properly breaking for commercials. Therefore, it is important that the other performers support the narrator. Even if the scene described sounds ridiculous or you are unsure why he or she set up a scene with certain characters, following the narrator's offers is key. Trust that the narrator will take care of you, just as he or she trusts you to make the scenes he or she introduces interesting.

Also, remember that it can be tricky to find the comedy in the dark. Create a character through your voice, play around with the fact that nothing can be seen, make a point to describe things, and find tension in pauses and volume.

The Coffeehouse Show is an open mike event that is part sketch comedy and part improv comedy. Before the show, improvisers come up with characters or bits and then individually take turns performing for and interacting with the audience. The ratio of sketch to improv can be different for each performer depending on his or her comfort level.

This character-based format is a great opportunity to try out a character you have always wanted to play or to build on a character you discovered while practicing. Characters from previous shows include a stand-up comedian who did improvised animal jokes and an Eastern European body builder who answered audience questions about fitness. This is a fun format that comes with built-in comforts. You decide how much to improvise and how much to prepare, and if you have a well-defined character, your interactions with and responses to the audience are easy.

More on Experimental Formats

These are just a few of the many experimental long-form formats. Some troupes like to do Shakespearean shows where the audience decides either comedy or tragedy and provides them with a title for the show. Other troupes like musicals or medical dramas, just to name a few. With any of these experimental forms, it is important that you as a troupe study them, do research (listen to a few radio shows on the Internet, learn what Shakespeare was all about, crash a dinner party), and above all, practice!

As you practice, you will find what works best for your troupe and you can modify the formats to best suit you. Perhaps for a Dinner Party Show you will want to have a character apologetically arrive halfway through or you will want to interact with the audience more. Maybe you want to do a Radio Show but without the comforts and constraints of the narrator. That is all fine, but you will only learn what is best if you practice each format. These experimental formats are meant to be fun, so play around with them and make them your own!

IGP PRESENTS:
Historical Improv Formats

1. The Telegram Show – This precursor to the Radio Show was hugely popular among the men and women in the armed forces, as coded improv shows were sent from the States to stations overseas. It fell by the wayside after WWI, but not before being awarded a Silver Star.

2. The Sausage Fest Show – This show was performed exclusively by German males, and it featured improvisers with bratwurst sausages that were used as props, but never as sausages. With the rise of the Roast Beef and Ham Shows in the mid-eighteenth century, the Sausage Fest Show became regarded as just yet another clichéd meat improv format and was soon forgotten.

3. The Scientist Show — This famous format featured scientists sharing their research findings with the public before being imprisoned for heresy. Galileo was famous for performing this show in his underwear.

A Brief Note about Musical Improv, by IGP's Pianist

J.S Bach once said that playing music is really nothing more than playing the right note at the right time. The secret of comedy, it has long been said, is timing. By synthesizing these two points, we can infer that a.) J.S. Bach was probably hilarious, and b.) music and comedy are closely linked. As such, combining the two fields seems like a natural and effective way to inject a new level of energy into either one.

In accordance with this theory, many improv troupes (and IGP, at various points in its history, has been one of them) elect to incorporate music into their performances, and to achieve this end, they will bring a musician into the troupe. The good news: if you are among the countless people who are not inclined to being verbally funny onstage but who can play an instrument and still want one day to be asked to contribute something to a book about improv comedy, this may be your in.

In the most general terms, as a musician in an improv troupe, your job will be to contribute musically to the humor onstage. In most troupes, this tends to involve underscoring some scenes, improvising full-blown songs where the people sing along onstage, and contributing various other noises as the show requires. The troupe's musician usually plays some sort of keyboard instrument, but that is just for the sake of flexibility. An improv oboist would do just fine if that is your thing. You would just really have to own it, the oboe thing. Though to be honest, it would still be pretty weird.

Whatever instrument you end up with, it is important to note that providing music in an improv comedy context is not unlike improvising with other musicians. You pay close attention to what the other players are doing, and you poke your head into the frame when you think you can add something to what is going on. It should never just be about you.

You will notice that this is not terribly different from what this book has been telling you to do as a normal, speaking, acting improvisational comedian. This is not a coincidence. Nearly all of those same improv rules (or similar versions) apply to musicians, and this affords you a set of tricks that are comparable to those of the actors and actresses onstage: you, too, can make callbacks, you can start a game, you can "Yes, and" (for example, "Yes, these two characters are passionate enough about each other to burst into a song about it, and it will be a tango!"), and you can easily tilt any scene by tweaking its musical environment in unexpected ways. Many of the dangers are there too, though. You can easily pimp, you can ball hog, and in some cases you can even block. Do not do these things.

The best musicians in improv comedy are the ones who think of themselves as another player in the scene: they are not there to show off, they are not there to flatter the other performers with generous song offers, and they are not there to ram a showstopping musical number into every scene. They are the ones who are willing to listen closely. The ones who are interested in working together with the rest of their team to make really funny things happen.

They just do it with a piano. Or an oboe, perhaps, if you are really sure you could pull it off.

Closing Thoughts

You should now have a clearer understanding of how you can format and present your improvisational skills. For those of you who want to do a show with both long-form and short-form games, we recommend that you do a brief short-form set (about five games) followed by an abbreviated long-form (about twenty minutes). It is not a good idea to keep switching between the two forms during a show. Any improv feng shui expert would agree.

And before you go off and practice, we want to emphasize that while it can be fun to explore many different formats, we highly recommend that you have a standard format that you regularly perform. If you are always changing what you do, it can be hard to become very good at any one format. Also, once your audience becomes familiar with your standard show, it is much easier to sell the "special" show when you have one.

In a way, a format is also a treaty between you and the audience, an understanding of what a show is going to be. The beauty of improv lies in its mystery, its spontaneity, and its unexpected and unpredictable nature. As long as the audience is onboard with how the show is going to work, they will happily go along with whatever absurdity grows out of the performance. So make sure the audience understands what you are doing (how a long-form format works or how a short-form game is played) and make sure you know what you are doing. Then practice and perform!

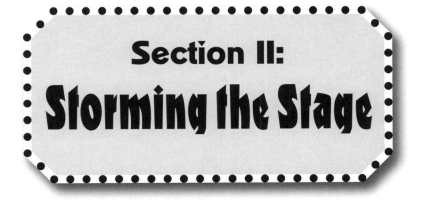

Section II:
Storming the Stage

Chapter Seven
LET THERE BE IMPROV: CREATING A TROUPE

The Immediate Gratification Players staged their first show in the back of a freshman dining hall, in a building that has since been renovated so many times it basically no longer exists. They "staged a kidnapping," grabbing someone in the troupe from his chair in the cafeteria and dragging him to one end of the room. Students began to follow to watch the spectacle unfold. They had no idea what was happening.

When they made their way to the back of the room, they found the Immediate Gratification Players standing there, ready to improvise comedy for the very first time. Or so the story goes ...

After learning about improv and trying it out in practice, you are probably eager to take your show on the road and get yourself performing onstage. Unfortunately, improv is not like eating a birthday cake — you cannot do it alone. This chapter will show you how to get some funny people together and form an improv troupe.

Birthing the Legend: How to Begin a Troupe

There are plenty of excellent reasons why you might want to start an improv troupe. Maybe there are not any troupes in your area, so the only way you will get to improvise is if you start a troupe of your own. Maybe the troupes that already exist are not particularly good or just do not fit the kind of comedy you enjoy doing. Maybe you tried out for some troupes you really do like and did not get in, but you still want to improvise. Or maybe you want to start one for no reason at all other than it sounds like a fun thing to do. Congratulations, that is maybe the best reason of all!

We will not lie to you: starting an improv troupe is hard. However, it is well worth the effort. After all, we remember a time when a troupe of irreverent freethinkers got together and started improvising a whole new way of doing things, coming up with ideas so radical and edgy that the powers that be tried to shut them down. Today we call that troupe The Founding Fathers, and they put on the biggest, baddest, and freest improv show in the history of the world: America. Are you going to tell us creating America was not worthwhile? We did not think so.

The easiest way to start an improv troupe is just to grab a few of your funny friends and start hanging out together with the sole purpose of riffing and making each other laugh. When you are just starting out, it may be a good idea to ignore most of this book, at least for a little while. When you are all comfortable being funny together, and that may take no time at all or it may take a while depending on the people you are working with, then it is time to start taking in the lessons from the rest of the book. (We suggest that everyone in your troupe buy three copies. Just because.)

Start with basic exercises that begin to build concepts like creating a scene, fostering acceptance, and playing a character. This might seem a little tedious, and you might ask, "When is our improv troupe going to start, you know, improvising?" Soon, we promise.

What you are trying to do here is build a solid foundation for your troupe. You are starting with a few funny people and trying to mold them into some sort of cohesive unit. Providing everyone the same basic improv education is important, particularly if some or all of your members are total beginners. You will hopefully already be on the same page from a team building perspective. That is why we suggest you work with friends at first instead of just recruiting random strangers.

Things might not work out quite as you plan in the early stages of your troupe's development. People may leave the troupe as things get more serious. This is not necessarily a bad thing. So long as your troupe is not in danger of collapsing, it is fine if some of your members decide the troupe is no longer for them. If nothing else, that is a sign your troupe is developing a distinctive voice that requires a specific approach to comedy. (Or it means you have become a bunch of jerks. But we refuse to believe anyone with the good sense to buy our book could act like that.) Structuring your group ultimately means you are progressing as a troupe.

Why start with just your friends? When you just start out, you are going to need time to figure out what kind of troupe you want to be in and how you want to approach comedy. You also need to gain some experience with what works in improv and what does not. Without that practical experience, you will not really be ready to hold auditions and judge the comedy of other people. Still, when the time does come to hold auditions, prepare for your troupe to make a major quantum leap forward. (We will discuss the audition process more extensively in Chapter Eight.)

Creating a regular practice schedule is the first critical step to the development of the troupe. Practices should not be overly long and stressful. They should be informal meetings geared toward making each other laugh and getting comfortable. Meeting once or twice a week, ideally, will help your troupe gain momentum and find a groove.

Whatever you decide, *stick with it,* but also be realistic about what you are getting into. Improv troupes tend to attract very funny people who are not particularly organized. They prefer making it all up on the spot to planning things out ahead of time. Can you see how it might be tricky to get a bunch of those people to stick to a regular practice schedule?

In the beginning, do not worry too much about the chain of command within the troupe. Do not make a big a deal about who is in charge and who gets to call themselves the leader. An egalitarian approach can work wonders for an improv troupe in its infancy, where everyone is on the same level and equally invested in providing feedback and making each other better.

Yes, there may be occasions when you need someone to serve the troupe — organizing auditions and shows, providing a place to practice, and getting the word out about your amazing new troupe — but very few occasions where you need someone to lead, at least in the beginning. If you try to introduce too much formal structure too quickly, you run the risk of getting away from what an improv troupe should be about: making people laugh and having a good time. This is improv, not student government.

There is still one thing we have not talked about: getting your nascent troupe to start performing. This is not an accident. Performing in front of a large group is a challenging, daunting experience, particularly for a new troupe. Do not rush into a performance because you think it is something you have to do to be a proper improv troupe. The worst thing you can do is put yourselves in a situation you are not ready for. Your primary focus should be on getting to a place where you can be comfortable with the thought of being funny for other people.

However, you may find that the best thing for your troupe is simply to throw caution to the wind and get out there as soon as possible for as many people as possible. That is what IGP did twenty-five years ago, and it is something to consider if you have formed a particularly brash, fearless troupe. But that approach is definitely not for everyone, and it is totally cool if it sounds a little terrifying. Some people jump in the pool, and some people waddle in bit by bit.

What we want to provide here is a basic framework for your early development as a troupe, a road map that can help you navigate and avoid the pitfalls that lead less fortunate improv troupes to fail.

You want to create a troupe that is fun and supportive for its members, but it is fine if some members ultimately drift away. You want to commit to practicing regularly without making the troupe feel like work. And you want to balance taking on the necessary responsibilities to make the troupe succeed with realizing that, honestly, nobody needs to call themselves "President" for the troupe to function properly.

In the end, find a way to take the troupe seriously enough that people remain committed to its success, but remember that it is just an improv troupe. If it is not fun, then what is the point?

IGP Presents:
Minding the Minutiae

We have given you the big picture, but there are also some relatively minor yet important things to consider. Let's say, for example, that you are starting the troupe up at your high school or college. Do you require official recognition in order to enjoy the full benefits and resources of your institution? It can be worth checking into, particularly if you hope to perform at your school.

If you are starting a troupe at a school, your group might require a formal adviser. A teacher or professor with whom you get along well should be willing to sign off on this, particularly if you explain that it does not involve any responsibility on that person's part other than occasionally coming to see your shows.

Also, even if you are a long time away from actually putting on a show, you should consider where you want to perform and what you would need to do to use that space. It might just require an email or you might have to fill out a bunch of forms, so it is worth at least checking out beforehand.

Finally, how high maintenance are you as a troupe? Do you need a motorcade? Bodyguards? The Immediate Gratification Players never take the stage without a healthy pre-performance spread of exotic meats. Also, one of our members is a vegetarian. And there is one who only eats eggs. Only eggs.

Who Are We, Anyway? The Troupe Identity

Once you have become more serious as a group, another strong element to your improv troupe's success will be crafting a unique group identity. If you can develop your troupe into a consistent brand, your audience will know what to expect from you at every show. Additionally, you as a group will know exactly what you should be striving for.

This means *consistency*. For example, are your shows free or do they cost money? If it is a scholastic troupe, are your shows on campus or off campus? What kind of format do you improvise? Is it long-form or short-form? Do you have any signature games? These are all key questions for which you should try to have a uniform answer, even if it is: "Well we *mostly* do X, but sometimes we do Y."

In the case of the Immediate Gratification Players, we mostly do long-form improv, with occasional short-form gigs for money. We never charge for shows — who would pay? And the majority of the time we perform on campus for the Harvard community, although we do hit the road to perform in other venues when the opportunity calls.

When you develop a strong, consistent identity, audiences come to build expectations of you as a troupe. We typically perform in one classroom so often that, when we switch venues, audience members go to the wrong place. And even though improvisation is different every time, some things are the same. For example, we always start our shows with a request for a one-word suggestion. Some audience members bring preconceived suggestions to every single show ("You never use 'tuna'! I always yell 'tuna'!").

You may also want to develop *standards* for your comedy, as well. In our troupe, we promise our audience a non-vulgar, non-offensive experience. Audiences can trust us to stick to those standards, and we also never have to warn anyone not to bring an eight-year-old to a show.

It is also easier from a performance perspective when you can consistently perform a single type of show (perhaps with added special shows on the side to avoid becoming stale). Especially as your troupe starts out, try to get good at a format you like. Your performances will be better if you a hone a single style rather than stretching yourself too thin.

Your identity can also evolve over time. When the Immediate Gratification Players first began to perform, their shows were completely different. From our extensive research of the historical archives, i.e. one phone call with an IGP graduate who was not yet senile, our troupe's early days leaned heavily on the murder mystery format. After the extreme violence of the 1990s, this format fell out of fashion. (We actually have no historical justification for why we stopped performing murder mysteries, other than that they can become very formulaic.)

As your group forms its identity, consider how it might complement the troupes that already exist in your area, in your town, or at your school. How are you going to provide your audience with something new, something different? You have to set yourself apart. In IGP, we like to say, jokingly, "We are the troupe on campus that does not suck." But that does not adequately answer the question of how we distinguish ourselves from the rest.

In reality, at Harvard, we are the long-form troupe — the other troupe does short-form. We perform a few times a month — the other troupe performs a few times a semester. Their shows involve their audience more — our shows tend to only ask for a single one-word suggestion, so our audiences do not give as much input.

Two troupes, two completely different styles. If you find yourself in a position where you are an upstart troupe, think of how you will distinguish yourself other than by "being better." It is not enough. Then again, if you happen to be starting the first troupe in your area, you get to define yourself without worrying what others are doing. Being the only troupe, however, does not mean you should avoid developing an identity.

If you want to be very forward thinking, you should relocate to Antarctica where there is no improv, laughter, or history of human settlement. Find a pack of penguins and perform for them. They are not harsh critics.

Building a Funny Brand

Improvisational comedy is full of famous brands. From UCB to Second City, theatres across this country have successfully marketed themselves to the public. While you are operating on a much smaller scale, your troupe must also develop a brand that an audience can remember. What follows are some specifics.

The Name

A troupe name can be a killer way to get recognized. When IGP was first started, its founders wavered between two names. One was the Immediate Gratification Players. The other was Soup. Needless to say, we feel they made the right call.

A name says a lot about what your comedy is like. Often, troupe names are bad puns. Take for example the Chicago-based improv group Mission Improvable, a take-off on the dated television series and Tom Cruise action movies. If your troupe name is a bad pun, an audience can come to expect bad puns from you. So think about that if you are thinking of calling your troupe: Could Use Some Improv-ment.

You may also want to think about how easy it will be for people to find your troupe on the Internet. Calling your troupe The Beatles is certainly ironic. ("The most popular band of all time has the same name as an improv troupe that performs in the basement of the recreation center? Hilarious!") But at the same time, if someone tries to search for "The Beatles" on the Internet, your troupe will not be the first hit. And probably not the second, either.

At the end of the day, a name does not matter all that much. Because our name is so long, people say "IGP" to the point where they forget what it stands for. But it can take your troupe's professionalism a step above "Improv Club." And if more people take what you do seriously, more people will be ready to laugh. (Counterintuitive, no?)

The Costume

We have seen T-shirts, jerseys, bowling shirts, jumpsuits, and neckties. Different troupes wear different articles of clothing. This can often be an extension of your brand. You may find it to be too much of a gimmick. This is understandable. But it does unify your look for an audience. When you storm the stage wearing identical bracelets, it may look weird, but an audience will at least know "They all must be in the same group." And if you are going to go for a unique onstage costume, you will at least be in the company of sports teams and symphony orchestras.

At Harvard, IGP is known for its red-and-yellow neckties, which people have termed "ugly," "garish," and "oddly endearing." We had originally intended for them to be a more stately crimson-and-gold, but when they came to us in the mail with a McDonald's-like color pattern, we stuck with it. Now red-and-yellow has become our color scheme and it is the most notable aspect of our brand.

The Gimmick

IGP met a troupe named Someone Always Dies, whose first few shows had a trademark ending, in which someone would always, you guessed it, die. We know another troupe that always makes a joke about Siamese twins in the middle of their show.

In general, you do not need a comedy gimmick to build your brand. Your audience may come to expect the joke even at shows where you are not interested in performing it — it can hinder you rather than help you. If anything, make the "gimmick" just that you are very funny at a certain kind of improv. That is the best road to success.

The Mascot

Your troupe does not need an official mascot. IGP has a mascot, but it is not an essential aspect of our identity whatsoever. Not every troupe worships a holy fish.

But we do.

Making it Stick: Forging Traditions

Much of the focus of this chapter has been on your troupe's external identity, but it is also important to forge a strong internal identity as well. This will largely be a product of who the members of your troupe are and how your troupe personality comes together. Over time, your troupe will develop traditions, whether you like them or not.

Maybe it is a pre-show chant of a football fight song. Maybe afterward you always eat a certain kind of food. These are the little things that will help your troupe to bond and keep it together over time.

More seriously, if you want your troupe to last, you may want to formalize some rules. Maybe it is a constitution, maybe it is a manifesto, or maybe it is just a motto. Creating a sense of institutional memory will allow your troupe to maintain consistency over time. Then again, you may only have ambition for your troupe to last six months. If that is the case, you need not sweat the big picture. But do realize that that picture is still developing even if you are not thinking about it.

A Band of Improvisers

No one should have to improvise alone. If you can find enough people who share your interest in improvisational comedy to form a *troupe* of improvisers, you are incredibly lucky. Being in an improv troupe is incredibly personally rewarding and also a great way to learn how to be a team.

Remember that not every member of your improv troupe will be perfect. They may even make mistakes onstage. Try to recognize that different people approach improvisational comedy in different ways. Some people might create great characters, while other people say incredibly witty things.

But that is the beauty of an improv troupe — each person has a different skill. And when you come together to create comedy, the result can be pure magic.

"WELL AT LEAST I FEEL FUNNY?"

AUDITIONER # 87

Chapter Eight
AUDITIONS: FINDING YOUR BEST

Every year, the Immediate Gratification Players are sad to turn away loads of funny people. The IGP "acceptance rate" has hovered between five and ten percent for a while now.

Like it or not, most people have gotten to where they are in the world of improv comedy by nailing a few auditions. Improv is like any other competitive endeavor, from bowling to watercolor painting. Eventually, it gets selective ...

If you kidnapped IGP and suspended us in a bamboo cage above an erupting volcano, demanding we reveal the most important part of the improv process, the answer we would scream over the roar of erupting lava is this: auditions. Above practicing, publicizing, and performing, auditions are fundamental to the success of an improv troupe.

If you are looking to join an improv troupe, you will almost certainly have to go through some form of audition process to get in. If you are already part of a troupe, auditions are your chance to bring in new members and ensure a healthy future for your troupe. In this chapter, we will examine how best to approach auditions, whether you are the person trying out (the auditioner) or the person evaluating others (the evaluator). After all, with any luck, you will get a chance to experience both.

Show Off Your Funny Bone: Nailing the Audition

Improvisational comedy is a group endeavor. As such, once you have decided improv is something you want to pursue, you will need to find a troupe to improvise with. Although we have devoted some time in this book to forming your own troupe (which is easily the best way to win an audition), most of you will probably try to join a preexisting troupe, and most troupes will ask you to audition first.

That means you will have to put yourself in a situation where, in a very limited space of time, you will have to prove to a group of (presumably) more experienced improvisers that you have what it takes to contribute positively to their troupe. You have to somehow demonstrate that you are not only funny but that you are a good technical improviser or at least have the potential to be. That is a tall order when you may only have an hour or two (or five minutes) to show your stuff, particularly when you are sharing that time with a bunch of other improvisers who will vary in talent and ability. So what is the secret to the perfect audition?

1. Have a Sense of Humor

Here is an answer that you do not need to pay money for: the most basic thing that you need is to *be funny*. That might sound insultingly obvious, but it is hard to ignore how important it is. At the same time, it is probably the thing you should worry about the least. After all, at a certain point, either people laugh when you open your mouth or they do not and there is not all that much you can do about it either way. If you have the refined taste to buy this book, you have probably been told at some point that you had a good sense of humor. We will even include a signed certificate to that effect, just so you do not have to question whether you are really funny. You can have that little bit of confidence for free.

2. Adapt Your Humor

Funny is a subjective thing. Your real challenge is to demonstrate that you are funny in a way that fits with the particular sense of humor of the troupe you are auditioning for. While the best improvisers and comedians have their own distinctive voice that informs their humor, you are more likely to succeed in auditions if you can show that *your voice is adaptable* to the troupe's comedy style.

That might sound abstract, but hopefully the troupe will provide you with some clear instructions on the sort of things they want and do not want to see. Treat every instruction as a completely unbreakable decree. This is one of the very few times in your improv career where you most definitely do *not* want to break the rules. If, for example, the troupe leaders tell you they are not looking for the funniest one-liners and to stay away from pop culture jokes (two guidelines from the IGP list of recommendations), then listen to those instructions!

97

If the troupe instructs you to do something that makes you uncomfortable — not just outside your comedy comfort zone, but actually something you really do not want to do — then do not force yourself. If, for instance, they ask you to come up with the most profane vulgarities you can possibly think of and you are the modest type, then that troupe just might not be for you. It happens. Go read Chapter Seven and start The Proper Manners Players.

3. Stick to the Basics

Although funny is in the eye of the beholder, there are some things you should try to do in any audition. If you do not know what those are yet, you should reread the previous half of the book, because obviously you were not paying attention the first time.

The basic improv skills we have been talking about are *always a good thing* to display in an audition. Accept your scene partner's offers, avoid asking questions, create a physical space, show range in your acting and character choices. These are all things that any troupe worth being a part of will want to see. Indeed, if the troupe tells you to do the opposite of any of these things, that probably is not the best sign. You may have stumbled upon a group of highly selective idiots, and it might be time to do your own thing with a different set of people.

IGP PRESENTS:
What Are the Basics?

Here is a bit more about some improv "basics," as if we had not repeated them too much already.

• **Listen and accept offers.** *When improvisers watch you audition, they will want to see someone whom they can play well. Even if the other people you are auditioning with are difficult, work with them. Accept their offers, even if they are bad, and mold them into something funny.*

• **Avoid asking questions in scenes.** *Improvisers hate scene partners who hang them out to dry. If you ask too many questions in scenes during your audition, it will look like you are making the other people onstage do all the work. Instead of asking questions, answer them.*

> • **Show variety in characters and physicality.** *Do not hold back. Show the people evaluating you everything you have. If you were loud in one scene, be soft and quiet in the next. If you were painting a mural in one scene, drive a car in the next. Vary it up as much as possible, and let the troupe evaluating you know you have a lot of tricks up your sleeve.*

4. Be Confident

There are a lot of little touches that can really polish your audition. Even if the troupe does not necessarily notice these specific things, they should be able to pick up on the generally higher quality of your audition. Let's start with confidence.

A lot of nervous energy will detract from your performance and possibly lead the troupe to question whether you can be effective onstage. But on the other hand, no one likes a smug jerk. Thankfully, there is a middle ground between these two extremes, and here is the best advice we can give based on dealing with auditioners for years: save your confidence for when you are actually improvising.

As you improvise in your audition, show that you believe in yourself. As for the rest of the time? Well, feel free to make a little small talk with the troupe, but a little respect goes a long way. Remember, the troupe is getting ready to make a lot of difficult decisions and reject way more people than they accept. As such, the evaluators probably want to keep a certain amount of distance from the auditioners, and they may react negatively to people who act as though they are already in the troupe.

5. Be Kind

That opens up a more general point: when in doubt, just try to be nice. Auditions should not be seen as a competition, and you are unlikely to get very far if your every act is meant to sabotage your fellow auditioners. Never forget, however, that this is inherently a competitive enterprise.

The best auditioners are the ones who do the best scenes, and the best scenes are the ones where the auditioners involved are focused on making each other look good. A good improv audition should feel more or less like a practice for that improv troupe, and what is more fun than improv practice? That should be your outlook, and the best thing you can do is just get out there and have some fun. (Well, that and all the stuff we talked about before. But have fun while doing those things!)

6. Keep Your Distance

That said, the audition is not an improv troupe practice, and a big difference is that you almost certainly will not know the vast majority of the people there. At the risk of talking to you like you are a kindergartener, be sure to *respect the personal space* of other people.

Once you are in the troupe, you can use physical intimacy to great emotional and comedic effects in your scenes. But you do not know what your scene partners are comfortable with, so keep a comfortable distance for the time being.

7. Be Loud and Visible

Finally, in terms of physical space, remember that improv is a type of performance, and showing a little bit of thespian instincts is never a bad thing. Remember to face outward and never turn your back on the audience. Avoid mumbling or speaking too quietly for the troupe to hear you. Sure, this might all sound obvious, but you would be amazed how many auditioners we have seen who failed to do even all these fairly basic things.

A Little More on Auditioning

If you follow all of these tips to the letter and you still do not get in, there may be a decent chance that the improv troupe just did not know what it was doing. (At the risk of advertising a book you are already reading, that hopefully hypothetical troupe might benefit from reading our next section on running a successful audition.)

It is not fun to admit it, but not every troupe is worth joining. There might be other troupes to try out for, or you can always just form your own troupe. If it has one thing going for it, improv tends to prepare you to deal with the unexpected. And honestly, if you are funny, show you know the fundamentals of improv, and show a healthy amount of respect for the troupe, then getting rejected would definitely be the exception. If you do not get in, then all you can really do is reflect on what you can do better next time and keep an eye out for the next chance to audition, whether it is for that same troupe again or another one.

But let's be optimistic and assume you got into the troupe, which means that sooner or later you will be on the other side of the audition, judging a fresh crop of potential improvisers. It can be daunting, but soon you have to ask yourself: how do you find the funniest people among a group of very funny people?

Harvesting the Funny Field: Running an Audition

Holding the audition process will require coordination and the ability to make difficult decisions. This can be a stressful and exciting time where you get to meet new performers, battle through deliberations, and finally pump yourself up about the bright new faces that will be joining your troupe.

In this section we will give you a sense of the questions you should be asking yourselves about what kind of improvisers you should look for as well as how to run a professional audition that keeps your auditioners comfortable and able to perform at their highest level. If you are still thinking about nailing the audition, pay attention to this section as well. As much as you should think about what to do at an audition, it helps to know what troupes are looking for in you.

If you are about to hold auditions, get excited. If you do it right, a whole bunch of crazy, amazing people will want to join your troupe and it is up to you to hold their fates as if you are a giant kitten and they are your ball of talented yarn.

Say Who? Know What You Want

Before you post that first flyer, email that first invite, or start to vocalize the words "We are going to be having auditions," make sure you and your troupe can answer this question: Who are we looking for?

Knowing what the perfect potential addition to your troupe looks like is key to putting on a successful audition and finding the best new crop of talented folk. Have you ever gone to a movie rental store (dated reference, we know) and spent two hours trying to decide on a movie, picked one out, and brought it home only to realize that you actually hate Timothy Dalton? Just because a man is in a tuxedo and holding a gun does not make him James Bond.

Similarly, just because a person is theatrical and spouting off funny things does not make that person a great improviser or, more importantly, a great improviser *for your troupe*. Each troupe is different in terms of format, style, comedic sensibilities, and personalities. Even if you cannot express it in a pithy description ("We're the troupe that makes poop jokes," *The White Pants Players*), understanding what the core essence of your troupe is and what you value most about each other as improvisers and group members will make the audition process much easier.

There are a number of key qualities that you should target as you consider your auditioners.

1. Commitment

First off, consider the issue of *commitment*. For many troupes, this may be a non-issue. Very simply, they want the best improvisers possible. If those people happen to be incredibly busy and only able to come to half their practices, that might be OK if they are hilarious. In the scholastic setting, IGP faces this issue when the funniest people happen to be seniors with only a semester left in school.

Think about how committed you want your improvisers to be and whether you want availability to factor into your decision-making. The Immediate Gratification Players do not have a coach — the older and more experienced members pass on what they have learned to the newbies. And with this approach, we start to view taking on new members as an investment.

In our experience, it usually takes at least half a year for new members to really understand our style and usually two years before they are at the point where they have both the confidence and understanding of their own improv skills to start teaching newer members. If we teach new members our style and they leave soon after, we have wasted our time. Thus, we typically target people who we know will stay in the troupe for the long haul — in our case, college freshmen. It is important to pick people who are very funny and very committed to being funny with you.

2. Balance

You also want to remember the issue of *balance* in your troupe. This can come into play in a lot of different ways, for example gender and race. But in this case, the most important balance to remember is age. If you want your troupe to last, you will want a mixture of younger and older members.

If you are at a school, you will want members from every class year. Because if your troupe is all seniors (or all senior citizens), it may not last beyond the spring. Keep the question of balance in mind when looking for new blood.

3. Past Experience

Another big question that comes into play when looking at auditioners is that of *past improv training and experience.* In every audition, the range of previous experience will vary. There will be everybody from the performers who started doing three-line scenes with their placentas while their mothers were in Lamaze class to the ones who have never heard laughter or known what a smile feels like.

As exciting as it is to see one of your auditioners trained or performed at a professional theatre, we have found that looking at someone's resumé is actually one of the worst indicators as to whether or not that person will be a great fit for your troupe. What matters most is what you actually see someone bring to the audition and whether or not that person plays well with other people. What you are looking for is that natural improv instinct, that raw magic that happens when someone is onstage working with a scene partner to create an incredibly engaging and hilarious scene.

People who have taken classes in the past will probably have better fundamentals than those with no experience. People who have never improvised before are more likely to be "blocky" or ask questions. A thing to keep in mind, however, is that you may be watching this person's first or second hour of improv *ever*.

If someone shows a spark that would be perfect for your troupe but perhaps is a bit rough around the edges, definitely consider taking the chance on that person. The key here is not to let someone's resumé dominate your impressions of him or her. If someone with a lot of experience is making really bad choices and not helping to build scenes, you may be looking at someone who has developed many bad improv habits. Bad habits can be hard to break. In certain situations it might be better to select someone with little to no experience at all.

At professional improvisation theatres, everyone who takes classes usually has to start at the first level and work their way through the fifth or sixth level before they can audition to perform. Similarly, when you do decide on the people you are taking into your troupe, they are starting at "level one" in your troupe. So look for that magic, look for that heart, and find that commitment to the values that you have developed as a troupe.

IGP PRESENTS:
Troupe Diversity

Diversity is worth noting when auditioning new people. When we say diversity, we mean everything: gender, ethnicity, culture, geographical background, height, weight, sexiness, etcetera.

While this should never be a deciding factor in a person's audition (well, perhaps sexiness), people with different backgrounds and upbringings can bring different senses of humor to the troupe.

Being raised in a different culture or even a different part of the country gives each individual a unique pool of humor, stories, characters, and relationships to tap into. Having people from different backgrounds gives your troupe access to all of those things and the combinations and contrasts when two great improvisers bring different experiences to the table is always ripe with humor. Imagine improvising with a troupe made up of just clones of yourself. The scenes would become repetitive and boring and probably deal with the same neuroses again and again.

Does that sound fun to perform or to watch? Keep an eye out, and look for those unique pools of humor ready to be tapped.

Keeping It Together: A Professional Audition

You and your troupe will want to have everything planned out for the audition process. Sure you can say, "Hey man, we're just a chill group of bros and babes who love to improv. Our audition process is super laid back and chill." You are entirely welcome to be as chill or un-chill as you want, but without a planned structure to your audition process, you will not be giving yourselves the best chance to view your auditioners' potential and make the most educated decisions possible.

Thus, you will want to set up a meeting before auditions to decide how they are run and what you will be looking for. While this meeting may be annoying to organize and thoroughly plan, you will be immensely thankful when you are sailing smoothly through the auditions themselves and can focus on watching the auditioners give it their all.

An important part of planning auditions is figuring out how to present your troupe in a *professional manner*. If you look like you are on top of your game and prepared for your auditioners, they will be that much more excited to show you their best comedy.

The key here is *consistency and fairness*. There is nothing worse than eliminating an auditioner because you made a mistake and did not give that person equal time to show his or her stuff. Make sure everyone is given equal amount of time in your schedule. Additionally, having a planned out, consistent structure is useful if you have multiple audition sessions (we usually have five different audition times) so each person auditioning can be compared on the same drills and scene types.

An Audition: Practice with New People

Each troupe will want to run its audition differently based on what it is looking for from its bright-eyed hopefuls. IGP has found the best way to run a great audition is to replicate what regular practices are like for your troupe. After all, if someone makes it into your troupe, they will be practicing with you nonstop. If you perform more than you practice, you may also want to make an audition similar to what a typical show is like.

We are going to take you through a bare-bones version of what an audition can look like, and then feel free to draw on warm-ups, drills, or show formats from elsewhere in the book (or your own mind!) to fill out and make the audition that best suits your troupe.

1. Warm-Ups

Start off with a group warm-up and a quick name game. Get people comfortable with the space and each other. Also, throughout the process, try to find a good balance of sitting on the sides and taking notes as well as getting onstage as much as you can to improvise with the potential newcomers. For example, with the warm-ups and name game, have your whole troupe mix with the auditioners. This makes the environment much more friendly and warm and keeps people from feeling like they are constantly being judged and inspected (even though they are).

2. Guidelines

Once warm-ups are complete, we have found that this is a good time to review what we are looking for in an audition. In IGP's spiel, we usually talk about how we are not looking for who can make the most jokes or one-liners. Rather, we are looking for people who can play well and help build strong relationships and scenes. We ask auditioners to play a range of characters and emotions.

Also make sure to note what you are *not* looking for. For IGP, this usually means no pop culture humor, drug or alcohol references, or anything that could make an audience member uncomfortable. The classic example we use of what not to do is a scene where Sean Connery is on the toilet, doing drugs, while on the phone with his mom who has cancer.

You can choose what to say and what not to say in terms of what you are and are not looking for. What we would recommend is advising people to be respectful of each other's physical space and to try to avoid any touching that could make anyone uncomfortable. Basically, lay out the rules that will help everyone be comfortable auditioning and working to show you what you are looking to see.

3. Basic Scenes

After going through the guidelines for the audition, go into some basic three-line scenes. (See Chapter Four on drills if this is meaningless to you.) After everyone has been through twice, start to extend the scenes and let them go for a few more lines. Have members from your troupe jump into a few scenes once they get going.

When joining in to do scenes, keep it low-key and use it as an opportunity to learn more about someone you are not sure of. One of the best ways to make up your mind as to whether someone deserves a callback is by jumping in a scene with them. Actually improvising with people gives you a great sense of how you would work with them and what they can bring to the troupe. Sometimes auditions come down to whether members of the troupe have a good feeling about their synergy with the auditioners.

4. Drills

After you are done with basic scenes, a good idea is to get into some drills that replicate the type of performance you would be doing in a show. This will vary depending on whether you are a short-form group or a long-form one. A short-form troupe actually has a much easier job as all you have to do is pick a set of games you would play in a normal show and then have your auditioners go through them.

For long-form, it can be a bit trickier as you do not have enough time to explain to them the mechanics of editing or how to go about doing formats such as the Harold. What the Immediate Gratification Players do instead is use a few games that replicate the types of skills you want out of a long-form improviser. These games are typically easy to explain and are shorter so that all the auditioners get an equal shot to go through them.

Using drills that target the key skills we have talked about throughout the book will help you decide who has them and who is sorely missing them. There is also no reason to limit the length of your auditions if you need to go long to fit everyone in. It is definitely more important and valuable to make sure you have seen everything you want to see from your auditioners before letting them go.

Typical Audition Drills

The Story Game: We usually play this game at the end of the first audition. It focuses on trying to create strong characters. Stand in a circle and have the leader of your troupe ask an impromptu question to one of the auditioners along the lines of: "Where were you when the building caught fire?" or "Have you always had a passion for gardening?"

The auditioner is told to become a strong character and then answer the question in the form of a short monologue while maintaining the character. This is usually a fun drill and an opportunity for people to show off their ability to think on the spot and take on a different persona.

One to Four, Four to One: For this game we take four auditioners up onstage and give them the numbers one through four. The person numbered one starts by doing a one-person scene all by him or herself. Clap the scene to an end and call in person number two for a two-person scene. This scene should feature brand new characters in a brand new setting.

Follow this pattern with a three-person scene and then a four-person scene. After the four-person scene ends, take out person number four and have the three remaining people revisit their three-person scene while some time has passed. Then revisit the two-person scene and the one-person scene.

Location Game: This game is about making a strong character choice and then being able to stick with it and maintain it across scenes. Divide your auditioners into groups of four or five. Get the first group up onstage and give them a location. The best locations are places where there would be a good reason to have a bunch of different types of people with different roles and statuses. Good examples are a school, a ship, or a farm. All of the scenes will take place in and around that same location.

Then call two people out of the group and have them do a two-person scene. In the first scene, they will define their characters. Clap the scene out, and then call two more people until everyone has done a scene and created a character. Proceed to go through the combinations so that everyone does a scene with everyone else. Remember you are looking for people who can maintain their character and find ways to build relationships and humor from their interactions with the rest of the people at the location.

IGP PRESENTS:
Close to the Chest

While watching your auditioners go through drills and scenes, you will see some incredibly hysterical moments and some moments of pure awkwardness. As difficult as it may be, try to keep your reactions and impressions to yourselves as much as possible.

You do not want improvisers to quit on you because they think they are doing poorly or realize that Johnny "Born to Improv" Jones is a shoo-in and fret about how that means there is one less spot for them. Politely laugh and encourage. This will keep people from becoming nervous. Also, do not fake laugh too much. The people auditioning may think the person who pretended to eat garbage onstage is actually a good improviser. This can become confusing.

Making Cuts: The Decision Process

With the auditions over, you and your troupe will move on to the process of deciding who gets a callback and who is going to be in your troupe. There will be a million things to think about and jokes to analyze, but if you and your troupe are on the same page, you will no doubt be able to come to a decision and find those awesome improvisers who will keep your shows rocking and rolling.

The decision process, or *deliberations* as they are called within IGP, will take time. Passions will rage, books will be thrown, hands will be gestured emphatically — just imagine *12 Angry Men* but with more rubber chickens.

Before you deliberate, however, we highly recommend doing a *round of callbacks* for your favored improvisers from the first round of auditions. Improvisational comedy is weird in its spontaneity. Receiving a second hour to watch someone improvise can clarify what that person would bring to a troupe.

In the callback, the drills should be more focused. All of the auditioners (including those with no improv experience) will be more comfortable with the process. You will see the nervous jitters disappear and their true talents shine through. A number of people who eventually got into IGP had shaky first round auditions only to blow the competition away in the callback once they had received the confidence boost of knowing they were worthy of a second look.

At callbacks, you should focus on all the first level basics. First off, are they funny? Are they good at accepting offers? Do they have a good voice and presence? Then begin to look at second level qualities such as range, physicality, and whether or not they "block" or "pimp." The first level basics are clearly required, as without those you just cannot be a great improviser. The second level qualities, however, can be taught. Consider again what you think they can learn versus what they will never understand. Take notes and *remember the specifics* of what you liked or did not like.

We will leave how you run your deliberations up to you. Needless to say, IGP has many arcane and meticulous methods for how we work through who will get into the troupe. We lock ourselves in a room and do not set a time limit. Eventually we come to a unanimous decision as to who the new members should be. Because we take these decisions very seriously and strive for unanimity, IGP deliberations are known to take easily ten hours, if not more. You may want to go for a majority vote if time is of the essence. But if there is one thing that we love about our deliberations, it is our concept of *unanimity*. For the current members of the troupe, knowing that you and everyone else have agreed on the next batch of members is incredibly exciting. It ensures that everyone's voice and opinions are heard and weighed. More important is the effect that unanimity has on the new crop of improvisers. Having them know that the whole troupe wanted them 100 percent is incredibly welcoming and makes sure that right from the start they feel like part of the group. If you can, take the extra time to reach that consensus, it will pay off in the end.

Conclusion: The All-Important Audition

Every year we reject more than 90 percent of the people who try to join IGP. This is an incredibly difficult but important process for forging who we are as a troupe. We encourage you to use this chapter to think about how you decide with whom you will be improvising. And if you are on the outside looking in, trying to join a troupe, we hope this peek behind our typically rather secretive process has proven illuminating.

Whether you have made it into a troupe or decided to start your own, the next step after auditions is building group cohesion. And after that, it is stepping out onstage and performing for the first time as a group. That is when you will know your audition process truly made the difference.

Chapter Nine

AND THE CROWD GOES WILD: A SUCCESSFUL SHOW

There are bad improv shows, and then there are worse improv shows. Sometimes improv will bomb — an explosion of silence comes from the audience. Symptoms include a crowd that does not laugh and improvisers who look and act nervous.

As much as IGP practices, we bomb at least once a year. What makes an improv show successful? And how can you ensure that you are successful every time?

So you made it through auditions and have put in the practice. Late nights, long hours, troupe breakfasts on the beach at dawn — you have done it all. You can reliably demonstrate good scene work, strong relationships, and great character choices. You have built a solid foundation of trust, and each member of the troupe is a pillar of funny getting pumped to raise the roof. You are ready to speed through the warm-ups and get into the game. Great! There is nothing better than getting out in front of an audience and creating some moments of hilarity met by peals of laughter.

The key to a successful show is in both the preparation and execution — much like committing the perfect crime. So before you head out there, you have to make sure you have everything: a great performance space, an understanding of your audience, a warmed-up troupe ready to go, and the chops to make it through a whole show. In this chapter we will talk about the work you need to do before and during a show to leave your audience's pants peed and faces wet with joy.

Warm-Ups:
Every Sport Has Them, Even Improv

Although there is no script to memorize or set and lighting changes to keep track of, preparing for an improv show still requires some work. Taking time as a troupe to come together, warm up, and collect yourselves before a show can reap great benefits.

A pre-show warm-up can come in whatever form you need. If you plan on bringing in some physical comedy onstage, make sure you stretch your muscles. If you like to employ a lot of voice work, get your vocal chords ready for some action. If you do all that, you will be ready to shout and jump without limping out of the scene in pain, unable to yell for a medic because you lost your voice.

Warm-Ups IGP has Tried That We Would Never Recommend

1. Cold showers
2. Energy shots
3. Slapping yourself silly
4. Truth or Dare
5. Milk chug

But more important than warming up the body is *warming up the mind.* Improv comedy requires an active imagination and ability to think on the spot. You will be much more ready to be spontaneous if you have practiced it offstage beforehand.

Individually, this can mean watching some comedy alone before you come to a group warm-up. Seeing comedy performed on the screen can inspire you to realize it really is not that hard. (Or it can scare you — do not watch comedy that is overly impressive.)

When you come together as a group to warm up (and you should), you should practice scene work based on suggestions from other members of the troupe — words you cannot plan for in advance. Schedule at least thirty minutes of this sort of activity before your show. But do not overdo it. You do not want to tire out your mind (or your body!) before the performance starts. Improv fatigue is a real thing; ask an improv doctor, who is definitely a real person.

Most importantly, make sure you warm up in the same group with whom you will be performing. An important part of improv is developing the group mindset, so if part of your troupe is missing for warm-ups, you will not be on the same page during the show. Build that chemistry — that groupthink — before you come onstage.

A note on stage fright: it is normal, it is healthy, and all it means is that you care about performing well. The beauty of stage fright is that it typically disappears when you go onstage, when the adrenaline kicks in. Unfortunately, this is not always the case. One new IGP member said nothing in a debut show and, when brought onstage to speak, took a piece of chalk from the blackboard nearby and ate it.

A great way to combat stage fright is meditation — center your thoughts before you go onstage. IGP is, unfortunately, only an improv troupe — and not a band of Zen gurus — so that is all we can really say about meditation. Try it. And if your stage fright is really debilitating (and it typically is not), you may want to seek out professional help, from a real doctor.

But once you have defeated your fear and after your troupe has warmed up, ideally you are firing on all cylinders and ready to do some killer improv. You are in the bullpen and the audience is making the call. Time to bring the funny.

IGP PRESENTS:
IGP's Typical Pre-Show Warm-Up

IGP's typical warm-up starts way before the show — when we get together to eat dinner. This way, we are accustomed to communicating with each other, we are already thinking on the same page, and we are chewing in the same rhythm. We also have food in our bellies — do not improvise hungry.

We then enter a classroom near our performance space. There, we do some stretching exercises and shake out our muscles. We practice very short improvised scenes and then gradually extend them.

Then we focus on building relationships, by doing a freeze game. Someone offstage yells "Freeze," the two performers onstage stop moving, and one performer is subbed out. The scene begins again, with the one performer remaining from the previous scene staying in character. The new performer can play whatever character they want, as long as the improvisers are forging a new relationship. Mother and daughter can become daughter and daughter's friend. And so on.

The rest of our warm-up is not that different from that of a basketball team. We yell and shout and high-five. And then we run onstage and perform improv comedy.

The Space: Improv in a Vacuum

Before you think about what you are performing, start to think about where you are performing — your performance "space."

The key to a great performance space is getting a feeling of intimacy and closeness with the audience. You are creating comedy together and you want them to feel, and be, involved. You want to treat your audience like a high school sweetheart. Throw your letterman jacket over the audience's shoulders as you look up to the stars. Tell the audience that you will always be together and they can laugh as loud as they want to; laugh until you go to different colleges.

The ideal performance space is in a location that is in *close proximity* to your core audience. If you are a high school troupe, that may mean a classroom or auditorium on your campus. For college troupes, lecture halls or larger common rooms in dormitories should be your go-to choices. If you are in an improv troupe in the real world, then you should probably perform improv in the real world — in a local community center, for example.

You must also be sure to think about the size of the space. The ideal improv venue keeps the audience *close to the performers* and is packed to the brim with people ready to laugh. That means if you expect forty people, find a room that fits forty people. A packed room is better than a half-full one, even if the half-full one is three times the size. Once you get an idea of how many people you can expect to show up, you want to find a space you can fill for every show. In a packed room, the audience feels more comfortable laughing louder — their laughs are not soaked up by empty space.

This may seem obvious, but it cannot be forgotten: make sure people can both see and hear you throughout the show. IGP has had some hilarious shows that no one enjoyed simply because no one could hear us. Make sure you are projecting your voice to the crowd and you have chosen a space that does not absorb your sound. If volume is an issue, consider getting your hands on some well-functioning floor or body microphones.

A final note on the space that we want to reiterate: take advantage of it. In addition to hearing all of your funny lines, an audience's experience is a visual one as well. A show can slow down and seem uninteresting if you are standing in the same spot onstage scene after scene. A constant challenge is overcoming the almost magnetic attraction that the wall you are performing in front of has on you. Get off that wall! Use all the space you can. Having scenes in different parts of the stage spices things up for the audience and often helps in finding new characters and different dynamics in scenes.

Using the Space: A Humorous Anecdote

A quick word of caution about using the most of your performance space: Just like butter on a piece of toast, there is such a thing as going too far.

At one point during a performance an Immediate Gratification Player was in the middle of performing an improvised song and started dancing around the stage and into the audience. He ended up rolling around on top of a grand piano, and, when performing a kicking dismount, he landed his foot squarely in the face of a lovely young woman who — up until that point — had been enjoying the show.

The message is this: if you do venture beyond the stage, do so cautiously!

IGP PRESENTS:
IGP's Home Court

Each troupe has different needs when it comes to a performance space. IGP's current favorite spot on campus works well for our audiences and for us.

After many years of shows around campus, we found our ideal "home court" – the Fong Auditorium in Boylston Hall, centrally located in Harvard Yard. The auditorium is a two-minute walk for freshman and a maximum ten-minute walk for upperclassmen. There are a number of adjacent classrooms that provide a great place for IGP to warm up before the show without distractions.

A regular IGP show typically draws anywhere from sixty to 160 people. The Fong Auditorium seats 144, so the space feels full. It is not the number of bodies that create more laughter; it is how full the room is.

Another great aspect of the Fong Auditorium is the fairly steep stadium seating, so everyone in the audience can both see and hear IGP perform its comedy.

Performing a show in a packed Fong Auditorium can be an almost magical experience, especially if the suggestion is "wizard."

The Right Fit: Know Your Audience

Once you fill the seats, you have to ask yourself who is sitting in them. Performing as an improviser for an audience is much like being a DJ for a really great party. It is about putting together an energetic set that appears seamless, but also constantly reacting to the audience and anticipating what they want to hear or see next. Before each performance, you need to understand what kind of crowd you are performing for and whether they want to hear "Unforgettable" or "Gettin' Jiggy Wit It." (These are two songs that are arguably equally dirty, but they have much different fan bases.)

Your main concern with an audience should be making sure that they feel *comfortable.* If an audience member is made uncomfortable by something said onstage, that person will be much less willing to laugh at anything else. You can lose an audience for a whole show with one comment. If you go so far as to offend an audience member, you may not only ruin that show for them, you will probably see much fewer people in attendance for your next show.

This is not to say you should always play it safe. Such is the nature of comedy — envelopes are often pushed and taboo topics brought to light. Just make sure you are doing so in a good-natured way that your audience is comfortable with and the laughs will continue to flourish. Of course, if being racy is really your thing, you can always try to get a new audience.

Relying on vulgarity to find laughter can also degrade your improv. Very funny improv should not come from stepping over boundaries. It should be from building great relationships onstage. Vulgarity can be an easy crutch and rather addictive. It is best to avoid it, just like crack cocaine. (See how cheap that reference felt?)

And lastly, keep in mind the expectations your audience may have. Different themes may resonate differently with adults than with children. Adults may appreciate a workplace scene more than children. Children may appreciate a playground scene more than adults. Gazelles may appreciate a fleeing scene more than lions. It is all about the context.

IGP PRESENTS:
The IGP Promise

IGP takes a firm stance and holds itself to a high standard when it comes to the content of its improv. We never use any vulgar language, make any references to drugs or alcohol, or address any topics that could potentially make someone in the audience uncomfortable (cancer, suicide, rape — the list is endless).

Not surprisingly, we have yet to receive a complaint for leaving these topics out of our humor. We are pretty sure the reaction would be different if we left them in.

The IGP Guide to Appropriate Show Content

	Funny	Edgy	Never
Children	A balding clown worries about losing his rainbow hair.	A clown decides to quit the circus and become a cop.	A clown is on the loose. This clown kills other clowns.
Students	A boy's mother puts mean notes in his lunchbox.	A boy's mother puts threatening notes in his lunchbox.	A boy's mother puts notes with sexual content in his lunchbox.
Adults	A man loses his job because he smells weird.	A man loses his job because he hates his co-workers.	A man loses his job because he has a debilitating illness.

The Right Foot: Starting Your Show

So the audience is packed in and your troupe is warmed up. You are ready for some hysterical improv to unfold ... but is the audience? The introduction to a show is a key moment where you need to connect and energize your audience so they are ready for the comedy roller-coaster ride ahead. It is just like when you meet an attractive guy or girl at a party — making a great first impression is incredibly important. You want that person to think you are cool, but not too cool. Hot, but not too hot. You have to Goldilocks it.

The obvious start is to introduce yourself. Who are you? Does your troupe have a name? What sort of improv do you do? What should the audience expect? A key mistake is to just say, "We're going to do some improv!" Many audience members will have no idea what that means. Clearly explain the rules and format of what you are about to embark upon. Let the audience know how they can help you with this mission.

Here is how IGP would introduce a show:

Hello! We are the Immediate Gratification Players and we are [All the performers shout their names]. Tonight we are going to be performing some long-form improvisational comedy, which means we will be taking a suggestion from you, the audience, and doing a series of scenes all inspired by that suggestion.

So, all we need from you guys to start is a one-word suggestion. On the count of three, shout out any word. 1 ... 2 ... 3! OK, great, IGP presents: albatross! (We would never accept the suggestion "albatross.")

That is a very basic introduction to set up a show. It can work well, but often an audience needs to be pumped up a bit more than only an enthusiastic introduction can muster. Other options can range from improvisers shouting at the top of their lungs, the audience being asked to get up out of their seats and dance around, or party music being blasted in the half-hour before the show starts. Some troupes use alcohol to inspire their audience — to questionable effect.

At the University of California, Irvine, we encountered a troupe that had (very impressively) created a cult following for their shows. Before each show, the troupe and the audience shouted in unison a five-minute long chant stating the rules of the show. Every member of the audience had been to the show before and knew all the words — that was a group ready to see some improv! If you can develop such a following, whether by making your audiences learn a script, giving your public some sort of challenge, or actually creating a zealous religious cult, *go for it.*

Once the audience is pumped and ready to start, you will have to *take suggestions* from them. That is, after all, the appeal of coming to an improvised performance. Not surprisingly, not every suggestion from an audience member is a good one. Avoid inside jokes, pop culture references, and proper nouns that are not immediately obvious. Prime the audience members by having them suggest something specific (a favorite place) before something general (yell any word!). And be careful when the shouts of audience members turn into one large noise blob. Catch the audience off guard by yelling "1 ... 2 ... 5!" and suggestions will come in more of an ideal pitter-patter. Again, know your audience and work to find what works for them.

IGP PRESENTS:
Viral Videos

When it comes to getting an audience's energy bouncing, IGP has had great success in creating sketch videos and then premiering them at the start of our shows. It takes extra time (and someone with access to video and editing equipment), but we have found that videos are a fun way to get the audience in the mood for comedy and also for the troupe to test out a different comedic skill set.

Writing and acting for a video from an improv perspective can lead to some amazing moments and lines and be a great way to practice the craft. Many professional comedians you see on television and in film use their background in improv to create honest and spontaneous dialogue, which often brings out the true kernel of humor within a scene.

Fast and Funny: The Performance

Once your performance has started, you will quickly realize that your audience is like a horse: it needs to be broken. There is a natural skepticism among any group of spectators; they have to decide if they like what they are seeing. That is why a fast, high-energy start is crucial to any successful performance.

A great improv show starts loud, proud, and big. Create characters that are energetic and move around. Do not start a show with your meekest offering — even if it is guaranteed to bring laughter at some other point in the show.

**To Do or Not to Do:
The Performance Edition**
1. **Do** laugh at actual jokes you see onstage.
2. **Do not** laugh at inside jokes you notice from offstage.
3. **Do not** laugh when you are onstage.
4. **Do** face the audience.
5. **Do** project your voice loudly so as to be heard.
6. **Do** start big.
7. **Do** vary the pacing.

Pacing is key in improv. There are both short, quick scenes and long, slow scenes in a long-form performance. Additionally, in a short-form performance, there are both short and long games — games that develop quickly and games that need time to brew. You want to alternate between fast and slow to create a rhythm that will keep the audience engaged. They should never be able to expect what is going to happen next.

In practice, you should try to *perfect the thirty-second scene.* This is how you should aim to start your show. When you receive a suggestion from the audience, it takes time to think it over and really milk it for all it can give you. At the start of the show, you do not have that time. Just go.

When you are onstage, you need to practice certain behaviors to achieve successful comedy. To repeat from Chapter Three, the audience has to hear what you are saying. Make sure you project outward with your voice. Be as loud as possible, even when you are whispering. A great joke that goes unheard is really not that great after all.

Additionally, never turn your back to the audience unless it is absolutely necessary. Orient yourself toward them, as they need to be able to see what you are doing. Keeping your face toward the audience is something that can be ironed out in practice. It means you have to make certain adjustments. For example, if you and your companion are fixing a car, it must be at the front of the stage, not the back of it.

It is additionally important never to laugh in a scene, unless it is fake stage laughter. For example, a guilty character might laugh loudly at a bad joke to try to avoid arousing suspicion. While cracking up onstage might get a rise out of the audience once, in general it breaks character and makes it seem that you are enjoying your comedy more than the audience is. One improviser in IGP who had a problem with laughing onstage discovered that biting the inside of your cheeks helps stem the giggles. Who said comedy was not painful?

And lastly, remember that the audience is always watching you, even when you are offstage. They take from you cues as to how to respond to the improv onstage. If you look glum or disappointed in what you are seeing, that is the way the audience will think they should feel. So be appropriate offstage and laugh along with what you see.

Remember, however, not to laugh an inappropriate amount. You might know the members of your troupe better than the audience does, so some of your laughter may amount to no more than an inside joke. The audience does not appreciate feeling like they do not get the joke. Do not make them think that way by laughing at something you see onstage that is not innately funny.

With a Bang: Finishing a Show

A common complaint about *Saturday Night Live,* whose actors mainly have a background in improvisational comedy, is that the sketches go on for too long. An improv show can suffer from the same issues. Improv is all about portion size. You want to leave the audience hungry for more.

That means ending each scene at the right time and then ending the whole show before the audience gets bored. Within a show, each scene should ideally *end on a "beat."* The way IGP has defined it in this book, a beat is a laugh line or a successful joke — each scene has a number of beats. In a perfect world, each scene would end on its best beat, its loudest laugh, although no one can predict when this will come.

Sometimes ending a scene on a huge laugh, even if more huge laughs were potentially coming, is healthy. It means you can return to that scene later and know you have comic gold to mine. What is worse is allowing all that gold to be excavated, leaving the audience staring at a crevasse, devoid of hope.

There are many ways to *edit* a scene, or cut it and move to the next one. In a short-form improv show, this can be very simple. When a game has reached the end of its run, you can yell anything from "And scene!" to "Cut!" and the game will be over. In a long-form show, when scenes run one to the next, this is more difficult.

In long-form, the typical edit simply entails disrupting the current scene. A performer from offstage strides onstage, uttering a completely different line out of context, which starts a new scene. As long as the new performer does not acknowledge the old ones, it is clear that this is a clean break, and the old performers rush offstage. If the new performer wants to involve one of the old performers, he or she makes eye contact or physical contact with that person or people so that they know to stay.

Edits are tricky to perfect and should be practiced often. If you are in doubt as to if you have been edited, just leave the stage. The issue of too few improvisers onstage can be readily fixed. Too many onstage is harder to make right.

A mixture of edits and scene lengths creates a varied show. Each performance has its own trajectory — at some point it will peak, and the rest is downhill. You need not end a show at its peak, but you must recognize when the audience's laughter is no longer escalating. That means your show is about done. IGP has found that a good show lasts no more than forty minutes. The same is true of shows on primetime television.

As a show ends, give back to the audience for having paid attention by reincorporating elements from earlier parts of the show. Stand-up comedians call this a *callback*. Bring back the funniest characters and most hilarious relationships. Mix and match what came before. Audience members will laugh out of recognition and feel immensely gratified for having made it the whole way through.

When the audience is tired and you have exhausted all your abilities, it is time to call it quits. Pick a *beat,* that successful laugh line, on which to close your show. Do not be greedy about picking one. Even if it is not very loud laughter, the audience may not be that amused again.

Once you end the show with a yell of "And scene" or "And that's our show," thank the audience for coming and exit the stage. Then give yourself a pat on the back — you survived forty minutes of thinking on your feet.

Edit with Care — A List

There can be many ways to go from one improv scene to the next, and audiences enjoy it when you mix it up. A few edits are listed below:

1. *Verbal snatch:* A performer "snatches" the words said by someone onstage by repeating them in a different context. For example, if someone onstage says, "I wish I could marry you," someone offstage says, as he or she walks onstage and edits the scene, "I wish I could kill you!" A new scene begins.

2. *Object snatch:* This is similar to a verbal snatch, except instead of interchanging words, you exchange an object. If, for example, a ring is being used at a wedding, someone offstage could enter the scene, steal the ring, and make it his or her superhero ring. A new scene begins.

3. *Wash:* Several performers from offstage run on the stage and break the reality with their bodies, often adding a "whooshing" sound with their mouths. The stage is reset and new performers can begin a new scene.

4. *Wheel:* This is similar to a verbal snatch, except that one person stays onstage while others substitute themselves in and out as the partner, reenacting a scene each time slightly different.

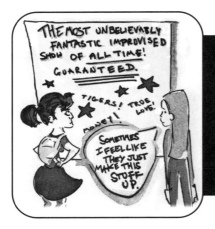

Chapter Ten
PUBLICITY: TURNING ON THE MACHINE

There are a number of ways to publicize a show. But the only publicity that you can keep forever is the flyer. And while great designs may grab the eye, more often than not the flyers you hand out will end up in the trash can.

Even if they are not effective, however, they are good for one thing: mementos. So make flyers for your shows. And then save them. Because when the memories fade and the jokes no longer exist in your recollection, you will still have that little slip of paper to say you did it, you were there. You improvised ...

There is a famous old saying that goes, "If a tree falls in the forest and nobody laughs, somewhere in the world a comedian dies." This is true 85 percent of the time.

This is a chapter about publicity. We have discussed so far how to perform solid improv, but presumably when you bought this book, you had the intention of putting together some great shows in front of big, excited audiences. In fact, packed shows are probably the best part of doing improv, after eternal life.

Having an Audience: Pretty Cool

There are a lot of reasons why you will want to get a really great turnout for your shows. If you can put the time into filling the seats, you will not be disappointed.

First of all, there is really no point in performing for an empty room — you may as well keep practicing in the basement. Having performed for practically no one on several occasions, we can tell you that it is much less fun and rewarding than performing to a packed house of excited fans. You are also much less likely to get a girlfriend or boyfriend that way.

Another reason you want to gather a bigger audience for your shows is that it lends legitimacy to your improv troupe. If you are attracting big crowds to every show, you have created a form of advertisement in itself. This is the psychological concept of "social proof." If people see other people doing things, it immediately becomes more attractive. This is what built the Pet Rock empire. Basically, if you get 100 people to come to your show, ten more will come just because it seems like the (right) thing to do. Large audiences, once you get them, are to a certain degree self-sustaining.

Additionally, shows with *bigger audiences are inherently different* from shows with small audiences. One of the coolest things about improv comedy is that it is one of the most interactive art forms in the world. When the audience is noisy and laughing a lot, it will actually change the way you perform. You will be getting a lot more (and bigger) laughs, the energy will stay high, and the show will be snappier. Once a room gets crowded enough, if you manage not to bomb, you can pretty much go into the show knowing that it is going to be killer. The bigger the house, the easier it is to bring it down.

We hope that we have sold you on the merits of audience. In simple terms, more is better, unless you have gotten to the point where the audience is so big you cannot be heard. But let's assume you are not off-the-charts popular just yet. Instead, let's move on to the topic of how you actually go about bringing a large audience together.

Building a Buzz: Your Onstage Product

There are a few things you can do to your show before you print a single poster that will give you a much better chance of getting a big crowd. Before telling people about your product, think about how you can make it as desirable as possible.

First, *make your show good.* Other chapters obviously discuss actual improv technique, but no matter how much publicizing you do, one of the most effective means of advertisement is word of mouth. So be funny people. If everyone knows about your shows, and also knows you are awful, that does not do you much good.

Second, it can help to *make your performances free.* If you are in a college or high school improv troupe, there should be plenty of spaces where your school will let you perform for free. If you are not in school, vie for some space at your local community center.

125

The great thing about improv is that all you need is a stage and some chairs. Your shows should have few expenses, until you start doing funky formats like the "Covered in Diamonds Show." If you eventually do decide you want to start making money through improv, think about charging for private gigs, but still have large, free public performances. This way, you can get your name out there and not penalize people who are coming to support you.

Third, *make your performances short,* and let your audience know they will be short. It is much easier to get people to come to a thirty-five to forty minute show than a five hour improv spectacular. That is just self-indulgent. A little more than half an hour is also a very natural amount of time for a fun improv show. (Think about the length of well-written, un-improvised comedies on television — fewer than twenty-two minutes.) Even the best professional improvisers in the world rarely perform for much longer than an hour, and they are both incredibly talented and have huge audiences.

In addition to keeping your shows short, you should have them at a time that will not conflict with other big events. In our experience, a great time for a show is 8 p.m. on a Friday or Saturday night. People are typically done with dinner, not too worried about their homework or their job, and have a couple hours to kill before they go out for the night (or to bed). Make life easy for people. If something is happening at eight, sometimes we will go on at seven and emphasize to people that our show is short enough that they will not miss their next event.

Fourth, *do not do too many shows.* There is a phrase in medicine that says, "Always leave them wanting more." It is a semi-obscure reference to radical theories about amputation in the nineteenth century. But it also works in improv comedy.

You do not want to oversaturate the market with improv shows. If you do a great show for about forty minutes, people are really going to want to come back for the next one, especially if it is free. However, you do not want to have so many shows that people will get tired of your improv. Your friends who are coming out to support you will start to feel abused and your more tangible fans will start to take the shows for granted.

That being said, you also do not want them to forget you exist between shows. This can be a difficult balance to strike, and it is something you will have to get a feel for based on your audience. Some colleges or larger cities might be able to support several shows a month, but some high schools or small towns might only be able to enjoy a few quality shows a year.

Fifth, *keep a regular schedule*. It can really help. By regularity, we mean both within and across years. It can be effective to have a regular, easy-to-remember system. Perhaps you have a show the second weekend of every month or once every two weeks. It can also be very effective to have similar schedules from year-to-year. The Immediate Gratification Players, for example, hold our annual Laugh Riot Festival and our Dinner Party Show at roughly the same times from year-to-year, and people begin to look forward to them and ask us about them before we even lift a publicizing finger.

Finally, *make your shows interesting* and keep things fresh. Rather than doing the same kind of show every time, experiment with different formats and interesting themes. This can be as simple as just giving your show a fun name, for example, the "Yeti Love Penguin Tour" instead of just "IGP's April 3rd Show."

Unique formats are another great way to attract audience members. Some of ours are mentioned in other chapters, but some other shows that the Immediate Gratification Players have tried include the Lunch Break Show, Breakfast Jamboree, Pancakes at Midnight, and IGP Presents: 12-Foot Ladle.

None of those are real. Yet.

Publicity: Spreading the Word on the Web

So now let's say you have scheduled your show and gotten your space and you need to put the word out. We will begin with by far the most efficient method of publicity at your disposal today: the Internet. Before ever printing a flyer or poster, make sure you utilize this low-effort, high-results portion of publicity. This is work that is much quicker, often receives greater attention, and never involves waking up at seven in the morning when it is twenty degrees outside to tape 100 pieces of paper to 100 doors. It is also much cheaper than printing out bundles of paper and paying for frostbite treatment.

The first way you can utilize the Internet is with a miraculous website they (currently) call Facebook. This website has essentially digitized friendship and personal relationships. You may have your qualms about this from an ethical or philosophical standpoint, but from an improv standpoint it helps you tremendously. There are several

IGP PRESENTS:
Improvising with the Stars

Once you have gotten your feet on the ground as a troupe, you can even try inviting celebrities to perform with you. This will draw you an incredible crowd.

The best advice we can give you in this regard is not to be afraid to ask. To improve your chances though, try to ask celebrities who might already be in the area. Work around their schedules. Ask them early, and offer them some sort of award or incentive. You can just make it up. You do not even have to have given the award before.

Who knows, you could be pleasantly surprised! The Immediate Gratification Players performed with Jeff Garlin in 2010. The HBO star became our inaugural "Immediate Gratification Player of the Year."

things you should do via Facebook every single time you have a show.

First, you should *create an "Event"* on Facebook. Make sure to include a snappy but detailed description of when and where the show is and how much you are charging. Then you should invite almost every Facebook friend you have that is within a thirty mile radius to that event. Facebook is constantly changing, and as it becomes more and more widespread, these events lose a little bit of their potency and seem more and more like spam, but in our experience, most people are still reading what events they have been invited to before ignoring or deleting them.

The other great thing about a Facebook event is that it keeps track of how many people say they are coming. This is not perfectly accurate, but after a couple shows you can use this number to help predict actual attendance. Make sure also to send a message to the guests the day before the show or the night of the show, or both. Last-minute reminders are definitely helpful, especially as more people have the Internet on their phones.

You can also use Facebook to have a standing *group for fans* of your organization. At first this will probably just be a group of your friends, but it may grow to include a lot more people. We have found that a good portion of the audience from every show is a repeat guest. It is a lot easier to keep someone hooked than to attract someone for the first time. With this group, you will have access to a select number of people to whom you can send messages with an expectation of a very high yield.

You can also use Facebook to turn *your own profile page* into a publicity tool. Your profile can become a giant digital billboard. This way you will constantly be reminding people of your show when they come to your page to stalk you. I know what you are thinking: "Psshh, nobody stalks me!" (Well do not be so modest! That is not true! We are sure lots of people stalk you on Facebook! We stalk you! No really! That thing your cousin said about your profile picture was so true! Your new haircut does make you look evil! LoLoLoLoL!)

On your profile, you can turn your profile picture into whatever image you are using for the event, preferably with time and date details. You can also post the event to your own page, make a link to the event in your status, and keep changing it frequently. This way it is more likely to show up on your friends' home pages each time they log in to the site, even if they do not visit your profile. (We are also assuming there will be new ways of doing this by the time you read this book.)

You should also make sure to *utilize emails* as well. Almost everyone pays attention to their email, and a well-crafted publicity email will make it by almost all spam filters. Just give people the facts of the show and try to get them excited about this. You can create a fan list to email regularly, or you can email other lists you are already on: "Hola, el club de español. Improv mañana!"

Another thing to consider doing with email is to send a *personal email* to many of your closest friends, which asks them to come

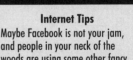

Internet Tips
Maybe Facebook is not your jam, and people in your neck of the woods are using some other fancy website. In that case, adapt these tips to that website. Your basic goal here is to hit a lot of people in a short amount of time on the Internet.

to the show because it would be meaningful to you. This is cashing in a few coins of their friend-guilt, so you can really only use this once or twice during your time in the troupe, but it can be very effective if you have one show that stands out as more important than the others. So if there is one show that would be really good to have a big turnout for, beg away.

An important aspect of having an online presence that will become increasingly necessary the bigger and more noteworthy your troupe becomes is a *professional-looking website.* A lot of schools host websites for student organizations, and it also is very easy to set up a website for free.

Make your website funny, professional, and user-friendly. Maybe try having a blog to keep people coming. Update your website with news from the troupe. It is always bad to have someone who is interested enough in your troupe to visit your website, then is disappointed that there is no new content. This is a person you want to keep coming back. Having a website will also help you immensely once you are at a place where you want to start having private shows for which you charge money. You can then point to that website as a business card of sorts.

The Internet is constantly changing, improving, evolving, and becoming self-aware. New ways of communicating are always popping up online. Emails have staying power, but who knows where sites like Facebook and MySpace will be in ten years?

What could the future hold for the Internet? Our guess is that e-cards will make a comeback. Do you think we will not put our money where our mouth is? IGP's entire stock portfolio is BlueMountain.com, which, by the time you read this, has made a huge rebound.

The point is, stay up with the times. Your fans will be a youthful group, and it is good to stay a little bit ahead of the curve. Your troupe does not need a LiveJournal.

IGP PRESENTS:
IGP Visits the Future

Before we continue, let us first state that this book was written in 2010, when the Internet was, we assume, just taking off. All our tips here are subject to change, though the intent behind them remains genuine. But if in the future telepathy is the only form of publicity, it is not our fault that this chapter seems unnecessarily dated.

Hitting the Streets: Traditional Publicity

If you are reading this book, physical media still exists. If you are reading it online, that is inconclusive. If a robot is reading it to you, they have already taken over and improv is probably dead.

But barring the robot apocalypse, physical publicity like flyers, posters, and newspapers can be very effective in certain contexts. Depending on where you are and who your audience is, you should consider including this in your publicity campaign. At the very least, as we told you in the introduction, they can make for good keepsakes.

Posters are probably the most basic form of publicity there is. They are a piece of paper, sometimes glossy, sometimes not, sometimes on colored paper, sometimes drawn in crayon, and they always include your basic show details. You put it up somewhere, hoping that people will see it and say, "Hey, I'd like to see some improv, doggonit!" Then they will come to your show, riding their steeds.

However, there can be a right way and a wrong way to put up posters. The right way is to not waste paper or energy. Put them up during the week leading up to the show, in places that are highly visible. These include bulletin boards, hallways, kiosks, the entrances of dormitories, and community centers. Some areas and schools have rules about where you can put up posters, so make sure you are not violating any of those.

Make your poster stand out! Often your poster will be surrounded by fifteen others, all for something lame like the Culinary Society or even lamer like the World Peace Foundation. You can make your poster distinctive by keeping it visually elegant. Omit all text that is not necessary to getting someone to the show. This is not the place to be verbose. Write a book with a chapter about publicity. Then you can be verbose. Bombastic even!

Put a cool image on the poster. Use something that conveys humor and excitement without trying too hard. For example, a picture of a yeti and a penguin inside a big heart would be a great poster. Yetis and penguins are improv gold. Use colored paper too if it is not that expensive. That really makes a poster pop off of the wall a little bit more. Do not actually do 3-D posters, though. People hate them.

Many improvisers will tell you that their least favorite part of being in an improv troupe is *handing out flyers*. It is difficult, it takes a fair amount of time, and sometimes people are rude to you. We can tell you, however, from enough personal experience, that handing out flyers works. It just does. You do not have to spend a whole day doing it, and you do not have to hand out a flyer to everyone in town.

Just station yourself in an area with a lot of foot traffic at peak times, like in front of a big lecture hall just before a class starts or in your city's downtown. Try to give a flyer to as many people as possible as they pass by. Many will not take one, many will take one and throw it away in front of you, but you will be surprised by the number who say "Oh cool, improv," or "I think maybe my friend is in this," or "I can't. I'm going to a bris." Handing out flyers might be tougher than a few mouse clicks, but if you really want a good turnout and wide community visibility, it is a great way to get access to people you do not already know.

You should also try to avail yourselves of opportunities to *appear in publications,* such as campus or local newspapers. Anything helps, and this is another way to appeal to a group of people who you otherwise might never reach. In a way, it is much more gratifying to have someone whom you have never met before come to one of your shows than to attract a bunch of your friends who will love you no matter what.

Getting Crazy: Creative Marketing

The last type of publicity we will cover is creative marketing. Two possible routes you can take with this are teaser trailers for shows and pranks. These are perfect ways to publicize an improv comedy show. They are a venue for you to showcase your talents and convince people that you are funny enough to watch for half an hour.

If you can *post a video* to the Internet and get enough of your fan base watching, this is a great opportunity to remind them that a show is coming up. This video can be a trailer of sorts for your show, though we would recommend not filming yourself improvising. Improv does not seem as exciting on film because it loses its spontaneity. Instead, film some sort of funny sketch and then forward it along to interested people in your community.

With a teaser video, keep in mind that it should be unique from other comedic short films. The goal is not just to be funny — it is to get people to come to your show. The video should balance comedy with energy and excitement. You want people to laugh, but you also want them to get pumped up.

One of the benefits of being in an improv troupe is that you have an automatic cast of players to include in the video. Do not solicit outside actors for your video. Feature the people who audiences will see onstage.

Teaser videos should be short, and the audience should not have to sit in front of their computer for too long to get to the humor. Try to keep the jokes punchy, and make sure the momentum of the video carries — music can always help out in this regard. Include relevant details about the date, time, venue, and how to purchase tickets, either at the beginning or end of the video.

Another method of generating publicity is through *pranks*. This can consist of anything! We as a troupe obviously do not encourage you to do anything destructive. If you kill a goat and spread its blood around some community recreation center and blame IGP, we are not going to take the rap. No way. We have been down that road too many times, friend.

Instead, try doing positive pranks. These can be funny acts that will draw attention to your group without making anyone think you are a bunch of lowlifes. About ten years ago a group of Immediate Gratification Players drove around Harvard Yard, our campus quad, in a truck on a spring day, throwing candy to everyone. We like to think that they were able to spread good nature and cheer before eventually being detained by security.

We cannot tell you what pranks to do because the whole point is for them to be creative and original. However, do make sure you do not do something that is too confusing or that you cannot own up to. This prank has to be traced back directly to you so that people know to come to your show.

Fair Play: Publicizing Well

We have shared with you many different ways to let someone know you have something going on. You can mix and match. Pick what you like and think will work well in your school or town.

Also remember that improv is fun. That is a large part of the reason why we do it. Publicity is not one of the most pleasant aspects of the art form, but it is one of the most important. The work you put into publicity has a very good chance of paying off. So do not be afraid to publicize yourself and be a little shameless.

Finally, keep in mind that a lot of your audience will just be your friends. They are coming out to your shows because they like you, they want to support you, and they think you are funny. Friends are the unsung heroes of improv shows. Treat them with respect. Do not send them five emails a day reminding them of the shows, do not ask them to do a bunch of publicity for you, and do not nag them or make them feel guilty if they cannot make it to a show.

Because, at the end of the day, whether people decide to come to your show is their choice alone. Publicity can only make that decision a little easier.

Chapter Eleven

SUSTAINING MOMENTUM: LEADERSHIP AND FINANCE

It was the summer of 1993, and the Immediate Gratification Players were down to a single member. Founded in 1986, IGP already had over thirty alumni, but like any relatively new organization, it had not planned for its future. And so IGP began to rebuild, one improviser at a time ...

For every improvisational comedy troupe that survives, there are other troupes that come and go. There are dead troupes and there are dying troupes in an improv sick ward.

Not every improv comedy troupe is built to last. Some last just one show — some are just a group of people getting together to make some comedy for a brief period of time. When IGP's founder was invited to IGP's twenty-fifth reunion, he incredulously replied that he never thought the troupe would last more than the four years he was in it.

In fact, in an almost Buddhist sense, IGP did die — twenty-five times. Each year's troupe, with students graduating and new students joining, is different from the year before. The comedy changes, the roster changes, and the only thing that remains is a brand and a certain way of doing comedy.

This chapter is about sustaining momentum. It discusses how to lead a troupe, ensure that your troupe lasts (if that is your goal), and maybe, just maybe, make a little money.

Take Me to Your Leader

Maybe your troupe is just you and a couple of friends. Maybe it is clear that you are in charge because, after all, you started it and, hey, you bought the book. Then you probably do not need a strong leader.

But maybe your troupe has more than half a dozen people; people you do not know that well, or people who were plucked from the community, like your school or town. In that case, it might be nice to have someone in charge.

For a relatively successful troupe, it may be too much work for one person to completely head up the organization. What with running practice, creating and distributing publicity for shows, planning a performance schedule, negotiating gigs, and finding funding, the logistics of making a few dozen people chuckle at your comedy can prove daunting for just one person. That is why your leader should be able to delegate.

> **Different Governments for Your Troupe**
>
> **Dictatorship:** Every decision your leader makes must be obeyed.
> **Democracy:** The majority rules.
> **Oligarchy:** A small group of leaders make collective decisions for the whole.
> **Divine Monarchy:** Your leader's parents also ran the troupe and your leader's right to run the troupe is given to him or her by God.

There are many ways to run a troupe. The Immediate Gratification Players elect a czar (or tsar, take your pick) every year. Call it what you want, but basically it is a despot who rules over all. Presiding over a land where all your subjects are comedians is not easy — it is not exactly a well-organized, put-together group. Below are three tasks that your leader(s) will have to keep in mind:

- *Running practice.* It can be hard to run a practice by committee. Someone has to decide which drills to run, which drills work, when to switch from drill to drill, and what to focus on that practice. Someone has to also schedule practices and harass (and even discipline) troupe members when they do not show up. That leader also has to figure out where to hold practice.

- *Planning shows.* Your leader (or leadership) has to schedule shows, finding both a suitable time and a performance space. Shows have to be publicized, and your group must hit all the right channels so that people know about it. During a performance, a good leader knows when to start the show, end the show, and move things along if they start to slow down.

- *Making it happen.* Do you want to perform comedy in another town? With a professional? Underwater? Someone in your leadership has to "make it happen." This person has to sell your troupe to the outside world and deposit the checks if money starts rolling in.

A leader has to wear those three hats; maybe in your troupe three different people can wear the hats (it does help spread out the hat costs). Some troupes have a producer and a director. Some troupes have a treasurer. Some troupes have no one at all.

You have to experiment to figure out what will work for your band of funny-makers. Some troupes find it better when no one maintains a central authority. There can be a certain collective irresponsibility when an entire troupe thinks that one person will do it all. But conversely, if there is no central person to lead it all up, the emails can go unanswered.

The Immediate Gratification Players do not like to preach, but we think it does help to have someone at least nominally in charge. This person should be a good communicator, someone who can stand in front of a crowd and say: "Hello, we are The Funny Frogs, Peoria's only improvisational comedy troupe!" In selecting this person, it should not be about who is funniest or who bought the most copies of this book. It should be someone whom people listen to and respect, and preferably that person is detail-oriented enough to handle some of the logistics of making performance comedy happen.

If you do pick a leader in this nature, it is important to let the leader be the leader. Respect his or her authority (unless that person would have you do something objectionable, like improvise over someone's grave). Make that person feel that he or she is in charge, and you will have a better leader. Some tips we would like to give to your improviser-in-chief:

• *Delegate, delegate, delegate.* There is too much work to do it all by yourself. Enlist your troupe members to share the burden.

• *Let your improvisers have an opportunity to distinguish themselves.* Impartiality is a key marker of success in leading a troupe. Leaders can dole out criticism, but they should always treat each member as a talented comedian. If you want the troupe to be its funniest, each person should know that he or she can succeed.

• *Do not do anything too unpopular.* Just because you are a dictator does not mean you cannot be democratic. Typically, unpopular decisions do not pay off in the long run like they would, for example, in American politics. If you take a gig your troupe does not want to perform, you can trust that it will not be very successful. Decide what your troupe wants to do as a group, and then make it happen.

IGP PRESENTS:
Abraham Lincoln – A Great Leader

Many regard Abraham Lincoln as the greatest president of all time. As noted historical scholars, IGP has condensed Lincoln's success into a few key traits.

Authoritative: Not afraid to let people know Ol' Abe was boss.

Delegated Tasks: Had a federal government system, which helped him run the country.

Communication Skills: Could read and write and talk real purty. He did have a squeaky voice, however, which is why he worked with a ventriloquist.

Beard: Who would not swoon for a tall man with rugged facial hair? All aspiring leaders should take note.

Making It Last

Maybe you want your troupe to die. Maybe without you, the continuation of an improv comedy troupe you were in would be meaningless. Maybe there are no Funny Frogs without Steve Watson, Peoria's funniest man!

But maybe you want your troupe to last. Maybe you envision your improv troupe as the second coming of the Roman Empire, lasting for a thousand years. In that case, you should plan for a smooth transition from year to year, without any stabbings.

Making your troupe last means *recruitment.* You have to enlist new members as you lose old ones. This means publicizing auditions and encouraging funny people to believe that your troupe is the best gig in town. If you do not take on new members, your troupe will eventually whither away. In the scholastic environment, that means having auditions every semester or at the start of a new school year. In the real world, it may mean having auditions once every few months.

One note of caution: it can be easy to watch a group of improvisers audition for your troupe and decide that none of them are "good enough" for your troupe. Do this enough times and suddenly no one will be "good enough" for your troupe because your troupe will not exist. It is much safer to take a steady stream of new members who you know will stick around for a few years. For example, not college seniors if it is a college troupe.

If you spend a few years losing more people than you gain, your troupe may find that it has to take a big group all of a sudden. This poses a much bigger threat to the quality of your troupe than incorporating a few members at a time, even if they are a little "less funny." Plus, any improviser will look a little less funny in the hot seat of an audition.

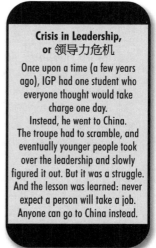

Crisis in Leadership, or 领导力危机

Once upon a time (a few years ago), IGP had one student who everyone thought would take charge one day. Instead, he went to China. The troupe had to scramble, and eventually younger people took over the leadership and slowly figured it out. But it was a struggle. And the lesson was learned: never expect a person will take a job. Anyone can go to China instead.

Another key aspect to troupe longevity is the *grooming of new leadership.* New troupe leaders are not made overnight. They are carefully constructed. If you have younger members in your troupe, make sure they are given important tasks so that it is not only the older improvisers who take care of the important business.

It is important to construct and cultivate institutional memory and to make sure it is passed on. New leaders should be slowly trained over time so that the transition is smooth. If you are thinking really long-term, consider writing down much of what you want a future leader to remember. The Immediate Gratification Players, like all Harvard student organizations, are required to have a constitution, and while ours is mostly a joke-filled satire that pokes fun at the pretension of the document, we do include more practical things to remember over time.

A troupe can change during the years, but it is exciting when troupe members have a collective history to draw upon. For example, IGP's leader has been called a czar for over twenty-five years. Hopefully your troupe can develop traditions that will stick around over time.

Rolling around in a Vat of Funny Cash

So you are making great rooms of people explode in laughter, and you are thinking, "Why am I doing this for free?" You want to roll around in a vat of funny cash.

Not so fast.

While improvised comedy is entertaining and audience-interactive, it is not incredibly easy to monetize. The Upright Citizens

Brigade Theatre in New York City — where Tina Fey and Conan O'Brien have performed in front of packed rooms — originally opened up in a former strip club and rarely charges more than five dollars a ticket. Do the math, and improvised comedy quickly does not look quite as attractive as, say, a career in trash management.

IGP once went to a college improvisational comedy festival at Skidmore College in Saratoga Springs, New York, where the organizers bragged that there were over 180 college performers in attendance. At Skidmore, we were treated to a show by a professional troupe from New York — the big city! — and watched people who were paid to do comedy for a living. There were 180 of us and four of them.

So keep your day job. For most people, improvisational comedy is a very exciting *hobby*. But we would argue that most artistic endeavors are similar — how many violinists or novelists are raking in the money? Improvisational comedy does have its share of Itzhak Perlmans and Tom Clancys, people who earn a high income from improvisational comedy. Typically those are the writer-performers who used improv as a launchpad to become Hollywood stars — the Will Ferrells and Steve Carells who pull down big paychecks to improvise in front of a camera.

Hey, that is the dream. But it does not mean your reality has to be one of stomach-rumbling poverty. Private improv engagements — for sweet, sweet cash — do sometimes roll IGP's way, and if you market yourself right, they might come your way, too. What follows is a list of ways to make money with improv.

The Celebration

If you are an entertaining group, you might be asked to spice up a celebration. Maybe an eight-year-old is becoming a nine-year-old, and she and her friends want to see some hilarious, family-friendly comedy on her *birthday*. Maybe a Jewish thirteen-year-old wants a really funny *Bar Mitzvah* party. The right parent with the right checkbook might want to add you as entertainment to a social engagement.

There are many situations where improv would not be suitable, however. Making jokes is different from playing jazz or singing something romantic. In other words, it might not be great for a wedding, although it is not out of the question for a very funny couple.

The key to scoring these gigs is getting your comedy in front of people who could potentially hire you, ideally parents with school-age children. (How many people are hiring improv troupes for their thirtieth birthday?) That might mean cultivating an Internet presence or advertising somewhere where parents in the community are likely to see it. One idea might be partnering with a local school (perhaps your own) to do a show for charity. Invite parents to come with their checkbooks, and you might be able to pitch your services at the same time.

Improvising at a birthday party is not as common as performing magic or being a clown, but it does happen and can be just as entertaining.

Going Corporate

Whether it is an office icebreaker or a team building exercise, corporations can sometimes use improvisational comedy to spice up the workplace. If you can find corporate gigs, you will tap into a very lucrative income source.

Often corporations use improvisation workshops to build their team because they recognize that many core principles of improv apply to the workplace. Acceptance and creativity are equally important in improvisation and in the corporate world.

To run a corporate event, you must adapt some of your drills so that beginners can take them and roll with them. Each drill should have a takeaway message for the participants. And the drills should add up to give a complete narrative that corporations can point to at the end of it and say, "This is what we paid for."

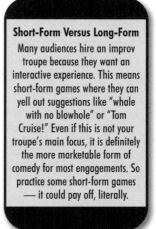

Short-Form Versus Long-Form
Many audiences hire an improv troupe because they want an interactive experience. This means short-form games where they can yell out suggestions like "whale with no blowhole" or "Tom Cruise!" Even if this is not your troupe's main focus, it is definitely the more marketable form of comedy for most engagements. So practice some short-form games — it could pay off, literally.

Businesses might want you for entertainment as well. Performing a show for a corporation can be similar to your other shows. Just be careful to not be crude or offensive.

Often, however, cracking into the world of business improv can be difficult, as there are likely already improv theatres in your metropolitan area for which corporate events are their bread and butter. And when corporations shell out for training, they typically go to professionals and not upstarts. That might mean that you should contact smaller companies to try to get them interested in your services at lower rates.

Charging for Shows

As a rule, IGP performs all of its public shows entirely for free. This is something we are extremely proud of. More and more in the scholastic setting, college and high school troupes do not charge for what they do. To their audience of students, it can be a huge burden to ask for money, and it is often better to ensure the largest audience possible by keeping your performance affordable. And when a show is free, it really cannot get much more affordable.

However, there may be certain situations in which you can feel safe charging for shows. Maybe you are performing in a venue that already has a box office, which eases the logistics of charging people at the door. When the Immediate Gratification Players perform in classroom spaces, it can be difficult to bar entrance and ask for money. Gauge your audience and decide what your priorities are: making some money or having high attendance?

Performing free shows is a luxury that not everyone has. We can do it because we do not pay to rent a performance or practice venue. If, however, you have costs to defray, charging for a show might be a great idea. You do not want improv comedy to put you in debt.

If your troupe runs up expenses and brings in income, make sure you put someone in charge as a treasurer who can ensure that checks are written and cashed. It can be easy when you are focused on the funny side of things to forget the logistics. IGP has performed for well-run Harvard departments who have taken months to figure out how to pay up. Make sure someone can perform the role of hound dog.

Price Discrimination

Ah, price discrimination: the only kind of discrimination that is still acceptable anymore. This means charging different groups different prices, and IGP has found this strategy to be very successful in terms of bringing in the most money from interested parties.

Typically, when someone asks how much IGP charges, we respond: "How much were you thinking?" Inevitably, the price the person quotes is much higher than we would ever charge, and we immediately say "Yes!" However, we do set a price floor that we do not go below. But this floor is very low ... shhhh!

IGP PRESENTS:
Mistaken Identity

One time, IGP's czar, whose last name was Black, received a call at 7:30 a.m. on a Saturday morning. Stumbling out of bed from his stupor, he answered his cell phone to hear a gruff voice on the other end. The man was a headmaster for a private school, and he wanted to hire IGP to perform improv for a meeting of headmasters. Being coy, our leader — whom we will call Mr. Black — asked, "How much were you thinking of paying?" The headmaster responded with an offer of one thousand dollars. Mr. Black immediately accepted.

When IGP showed up to the venue, they found 1,000 inebriated headmasters who were ready for some entertainment. The room was cavernous, and there were no microphones. The show was a disaster, but there was a clear lesson: always ask about acoustics before you agree to perform a gig. If the audience is more than fifty people, you should immediately worry about whether or not they will be able to hear you adequately.

After the show, the headmaster came up to pay IGP. "So which one of you is Black?" the headmaster shouted to the troupe.

IGP's only African-American member (at the time) timidly raised his hand.

Money: Why We Like It

Suppose your troupe rakes in the big bucks, and you do not all immediately need it to feed your eight children. Suppose you only have one kid, and he has already eaten lunch. What do you do with the cash?

There are many reasons that an improv troupe would *need* money, besides renting a venue to perform in or eating a team dinner. Below are a few ways you could decide to spend your funds.

Development

The best way you can use money you make performing improv is to *get better at it*. Improv comedians have a great ability to charge each other money to perform or learn comedy. If you have the money, pay for a workshop from a professional comedian. These can be tremendously rewarding, and you can learn much more in person than you can learn from a book. (Boo to us!)

If paying for a workshop is too expensive, go buy some tickets to see local improvised comedy shows. Watching other people perform, and thus seeing examples of what to do and not to do, can really improve your improvisation. It is helpful to see people perform on a regular basis to understand what is going on in the improv community. And if you see a particular strategy work well onstage, go ahead and steal it! That is free.

Top Four Strangest Gigs

The Immediate Gratification Players have been asked to ...

1. Hang out at a party as regular people, but be entertaining and naturally charming. Surprisingly difficult!
2. Perform for a boyfriend and girlfriend on her birthday. He paid IGP on the spot and then days later, the couple split.
3. Improvise for a group of accountants who were celebrating the fact that they had finished their work a few weeks early.
4. Act out "typical scenarios" a Harvard freshman would face. Harvard administrators asked us to do this in front of freshman parents — in Harvard's biggest theatre.

Performance

You can also use your funds to finance a performance out of town. Roll into the car and take your show on the road. Some of IGP's best performances have been out of our comfort zone — in a different state where we knew no one and there were no expectations. You can team up with local troupes wherever you travel in order to have a local, built-in audience. (Is there an improv troupe in Cancun?) These trips cost money, however, whether it is paying to perform or for somewhere to sleep. It can help to have some troupe money to subsidize these efforts.

If you are heading out of town, try to attend an improv festival somewhere. While some are highly selective, many are open to all for the right amount of money. Improv festivals typically combine a performance element with some professional development, workshops for example. They can be a great way to meet and learn from other improvisers. If no festival exists near you, create your own! This can even be a moneymaking opportunity. For example, IGP's Laugh Riot Festival began in 1999.

You might also want to use your money to fund a special show for a *local* audience. If you have dreamed of having a dinner party show but were never able to pay for the dinner, money your troupe earns can come in handy. Additionally, you may have a show idea that requires some special costumes or props. If you cannot get these for free, the only alternative is, you guessed it, *money*.

Gear

Your troupe funds may also go toward building the brand. Maybe you want troupe T-shirts (or red-and-yellow neckties). No matter what you think your troupe would look sharp in, customized gear is never free. A unified look can really add to the professionalism of your troupe and may be a good investment.

Other troupe investments that are inexpensive but valuable include building a website (typically cheap if your website is not highly trafficked) and taking group photos (for which you do not necessarily need a professional). If people believe your troupe is worth something, they will be willing to pay you something. It might make sense to plunge some money back into your group if you earn it.

Leadership and Finance: The Bottom Line

Improv does not have to be a serious business with a Chairman of the Board, a VP of Marketing, and a Chief Financial Officer. But if you do want to take your troupe to the next level, you have to think about leadership and finance. It might not be very fun, but it can really expand your opportunities to endure and thrive.

Not every improv troupe gets flown to Aruba to perform comedy for a large multinational corporation. (We actually think this has probably never happened, though we are open to any offers.) But the more seriously you take the endeavor, the larger the opportunities you will find falling into your lap.

Chapter Twelve
BUILDING A TEAM: HAVING FUN WHILE BEING FUNNY

Improvisational comedy, unlike some other forms of art, is about building a community. It does not prioritize the individual, it prioritizes the group.

The tighter your group bonds together, the funnier you will be. So spend time together and make memories. Because if your improv troupe does not have a whole host of inside jokes, if your improv troupe does not have a hilarious collective consciousness, if your improv troupe does not laugh together offstage, then you should really think about joining a new one...

This book has been full of rules. There were dos and don'ts. There were tips and tricks. There were commands and suggestions. We even talked about leadership and finance. But while we may have said it before, we have not yet emphasized the most important rule by far of improv comedy: *If you are not having fun, something has gone terribly wrong.*

Because improv comedy should be fun, so much fun that you should be dehydrated from all the fun tears you cried. And while fine-tuning the craft and striving for comedic excellence certainly require work, improv should never stop being enjoyable.

This chapter is all about finding the fun while you find the funny. If you are reading this because you have joined or are planning to start your own scholastic improv troupe, this especially applies to you. There is no point in pursuing something you do not enjoy, especially while you are in school. Let's face it, one in a million improvisers will turn their passion into a lucrative career, so you should probably have another reason in mind for pursuing improv comedy. We suggest the pure joy of it all.

Friendship: Why We Like It

While you probably do not need to be convinced why it is important for an improv troupe to have fun together, that is not going to stop us from giving you reasons why.

First, we have stated it before and we will state it again: improv is all about *trust*. The team aspect of improv is really what sets it apart. When you are on stage with someone, you depend on that person to be a good scene partner, and you are putting a lot of faith in him or her not to destroy the scene. And while much of that comes from knowing that the person has studied improv, it also comes from knowing him or her personally.

The relationship between you and your scene partner is much like that of a patient and a surgeon. Your partner holds your life in his or her hands. But also, you hold your partner's life in your hands, so you are also a surgeon. It is like two surgeons operating on each other. With no anesthetic. Or medical degrees.

You depend on your scene partner to accept your offers and add to them. The better your relationship with your fellow improviser, the more comfortable you will be to make offers because you know they will be supported. If you can trust your friend to selflessly make you seem like the funniest person alive, they can trust you will be doing the same for them. Thus, the better you can rely on someone offstage, the better you will be able to rely on that person onstage.

Not surprisingly, the second reason why you should like your scene partners is that it often leads to *better improv*. Some of the best improv scenes we have done in our lives have been with some of our closest friends. Fun, positive energy happens very naturally when you are doing improv comedy with your friends, and that is how you end up with golden scenes like two lifeguards trying to escape from a giant milk shake. The audience will recognize this energy and appreciate it.

When you are friends who seem to enjoy each other's company, you will be better able to anticipate what your scene partner is thinking and what he or she wants to do in a scene. Often, you will both discover the scene's direction before the audience does, and when you talk about the scene after the show, you will both say, "I was thinking exactly the same thing!" Then you will lean in and go for a big kiss.

This melding of comedic minds sounds mysterious, but it is actually quite natural. And it will happen quite easily over time, especially if you are good friends with your fellow improvisers and often rub craniums in counter-clockwise motions.

This leads to the third reason for befriending your fellow improvisers: hanging out together builds *comedic chemistry*. This may sound a lot like reasons we have stated previously, but what we are specifically discussing here is the development of a style of comedy that is unique to your troupe. When you hang out together as an improv troupe, your conversation will inevitably deteriorate (or elevate, depending on your perspective) into joke-making. Together you will develop a style of comedy that is all your own, which has its roots in your personal interactions.

It can be worth noting that while a collective comedic identity is definitely healthy, it does not mean that you should abandon or lose your unique individual style. There are so many styles of comedy, and what everyone individually brings to the comedy table makes your improv troupe special. It is the diversity of everyone's separate skills that makes scenes interesting, while the group's comedic identity holds everything together and provides direction. Both the individual and the collective identities are important, but while the individual style is pre-programmed into your improv DNA, the group dynamic can only be fostered through interaction. (This has been an improv science lecture.)

Lastly, from a practical standpoint, if you take improv seriously, you are going to be spending a lot of time already with your group. If you are practicing and performing a couple hours a week, you will enjoy yourself a lot more in general if you are with people you like. Also, the more the people in your troupe like one another, the more invested they will be in the success of the team, and they will put more effort into all aspects of the troupe.

A troupe that laughs together offstage will create more laughs onstage. If you are not already friends with the rest of your troupe, now is a great time to start.

Building Bridges: Troupe Bonding

So how exactly do you make friends with the people in your troupe? You might think you do not need the advice of a bunch of college comedians on how to make friends, and you are actually completely right. However, we do have some pointers for the unique challenge of team building within an improv troupe.

1. *Make the actual practices and performances fun.* The dynamic of a troupe that has no director is always complicated. (We will assume you have no director since many troupes do not, but this applies even if you do.) Because you have no creative leader, you have to make improvements by self-criticism. This is often awkward, as none of you have any real authority over one another.

Keep things light though. Foster a group attitude where people are comfortable calling each other out, always in a polite way. If there is an understood system for commenting on scenes, then people will be more comfortable both giving and receiving feedback.

2. *Check in with each other.* Be willing to sacrifice a few minutes at the beginning of practice to let people catch up and tell stories about their week. These "check-ins" are a great opportunity to share what is going on in your life and keep up to date on the lives of others.

We find that our pre-practice conversations are dominated by ridiculous and funny stories that always seem to begin with, "So this crazy thing happened to me the other day ... " and end with, "And afterward, I said, 'I have to tell IGP about this. They would appreciate it.'"

3. *Eat meals together.* Once practice is over, spend some time together. We often have a team dinner after our Sunday afternoon practices, which builds cohesion outside of the improv arena.

This does not have to be an expensive endeavor. In fact, it is often best when it is cheap. It is more inclusive and laid-back, not unlike how comedy should be. Order a pizza or go to a late-night restaurant together as a group.

4. *Have a regular hangout time.* This can almost be as important as a set practice time. After you pick a time and a place that works for most people and it becomes an established, weekly event, it is likely that you will consistently have good attendance.

For us, our weekly hangout is scheduled around our favorite television comedy lineup, although after the shows we often end up hanging out for hours watching movies, talking, and eating food. This is something you will hopefully end up looking forward to just as much as improvising.

When it comes to watching movies, good ones are fine, but if you are really looking for a rip-roaring good time (or even just an above average time), we recommend watching a movie that is incredibly, incredibly bad. Unintentional comedies are often the best kind.

5. *Set up an email list.* An active email list is a great idea for any improv troupe. It gets your mind meld going and stimulates the creative juices. Spam the list with your favorite videos, funny anecdotes, and ideas for group outings. Let email chains turn into extended inside jokes.

6. *Improv party time!* After a show, celebrate together as a group and throw some sort of event. This can be relatively low-key and have troupe members only, or it can be a larger party-of-the-century kind of affair. Improvisers are typically the life of the party, as they are funny, interesting, and talented dancers.

7. *Take group outings.* The next time you plan to do something fun, think of doing it with your improv troupe. These may be small-scale endeavors or grand adventures of an epic nature.

Besides movies, concerts, shows, bowling alleys, nature walks, and small-scale vandalism, the best thing you can do as a group is to go see some improvised comedy. You will be financially supporting people whose cause you share, and you may learn something along the way.

8. *Build the clubhouse of your dreams.* This is similar to a fort for young children, but is instead much funnier and more expensive. We recommend a building that is two to three stories tall with a nice black-box performance space. This clubhouse will double as a space where you can hold your weekly hangouts and wild parties. Most clubhouses, it should be noted, are entirely contingent on stumbling upon millions of dollars or inducting a member of foreign royalty into your troupe. (There will be more on this in the next chapter.)

Leaving the Nest: The Improv Trip

You may also want to think about a large-scale bonding trip. This means venturing out of town as a group. IGP has been blessed to have its fair share of traveling adventures, going to New York City, Chicago, and Los Angeles to perform comedy.

These are undoubtedly some of the funniest experiences you will ever have. That being said, these trips come with some serious logistical challenges. For major traveling adventures, there are a few things you want to take into consideration.

1. *When do you want to go?* Fortunately, if you are in a high school or college improv troupe, you will all have similar school schedules. The best answer will be to travel during a break or a long

IGP PRESENTS:
Start Them Young

Particularly important to cultivating a fun social scene within your troupe is immediately indoctrinating and involving the newer and younger members of the troupe. This is how you can progress from being a loosely connected group of friends to having a real group culture and soul.

The more new members enter into a happy, unified group, the more they will immediately pick up on that mentality. And the more effort you put in to making the newbies feel at-home, the more they will feel comfortable hanging out with you and asserting themselves in shows and performances.

In order to achieve this, make sure you are already hanging out as a group so the new members understand that these practices are established. Then, embrace the new members and they will fit in immediately. Be excited about them (that should not be hard) and they will quickly become active and contributing members of your group.

weekend. If you are living life in the real world, a weekend trip (to somewhere not too far away) may be your best bet.

2. *How will you pay for this trip?* Unfortunately, you probably have no money. Neither did we until we wrote a book that sold one million copies. And then another million when it was translated into Spanish.

Regardless, there are ways to travel without having a ton of money. If you are at school, you may be eligible to apply for a travel grant. To help ensure funding, use impressive phrases in your application, like "synergy," "the vanishing thoughtfulness of youth," and "improvised national tournament." Especially if you are going to be performing some improv, taking some workshops, or participating in a festival or competition, you may be able to get the school to help you out financially.

Another way to pay for travel is from the troupe's own bank account. If you have made money by performing in private shows, maybe you can afford the gas money to drive half an hour down the road and then come back. Or do not come back. Become nomadic improvisers.

If you do have to pay for the trip as individuals, try to make it as affordable for everyone as possible. You may want to practice a form of social welfare by having only the neediest in your troupe dip from the troupe's bank account, if it is not very large. Trips are the most enjoyable when everyone gets to go. Inclusiveness is extremely important, especially when you go on the road.

3. *Where should you go?* Go somewhere where you know people or where you live when you are not in school. Again, this may make more sense for a scholastic group. If you go someplace where you can all stay in a house instead of in hotel rooms, you will be saving a lot of money. If that does not work, get as few hotel rooms as possible. Against the better wishes of the fire code, put six or seven people to a room — you get close, fast.

Apart from that, seek out established improv festivals, where improv will be in the air and you will grow as a troupe. If you can, watch some improv, as it is good to see a variety of different improvisers. Also, do some performing. This is an opportunity to showcase your own brand of improv for a new audience and in new venues.

4. *What should you do besides improv?* Leave plenty of time to just hang out. The best improv trips are not business trips. They are just you and your troupe, being funny and having fun. Play games, engage in ridiculous debate, drive slowly, and blast music. It will be a hoot.

IFFL: Improv Friends for Life

You know how to have fun with your friends. You do not need us to tell you how. What we hope you gained from this final chapter of our book is a sense of the importance of having fun with your troupe. There are many suggestions for ways to do that here, but we are sure you will figure out a system that works best for you.

What is important, however, is that you make chemistry a priority for your group. If you do, you will always get more out of improv than you put in, both in terms of the quality of your humor and the quality of your life.

Your improv troupe should be about so much more than just improv. We cannot tell you how important it is for our group to be a tight-knit family of improvisers. We are funny, we have fun, and we love each other. That is pretty much all anyone can ask for from a group of amateur improvisers. We wish you the same.

Afterword

by Nicholas Stoller

Writer/Director of *Get Him to the Greek*
Director of *Forgetting Sarah Marshall*
Writer of *Yes Man* and *Fun with Dick and Jane*

I chose the Immediate Gratification Players for two simple reasons. I wanted to try improv comedy. And at the time you didn't have to audition. The troupe reflected this laissez-faire membership theory. I remember during one show a rather long-haired gentlemen, who didn't bathe and who none of us really enjoyed sharing the stage with, walked onstage. No one joined him so he forcibly grabbed me by the hair and yanked me. Not a pretend improv yank, but a real hair yank. Then we all got drunk on generic cola and vodka from plastic bottles. It was awesome.

Well since then IGP has turned into a far more ambitious and excellent improv group.

I did improv because it was a way for me and my friends to blow off steam and act silly. But in the course of my four years doing improv, I learned five incredibly important things about comedy that have stayed with me through the years:

1. The written joke often fails when performed onstage. That's where improv comes in.
2. The best comedy comes from character.
3. When you cede the spotlight the scene just gets better.
4. Wombats aren't funny. I'm sorry. But they just aren't.
5. Don't make your girlfriend or boyfriend attend too many of your improv shows. Like maybe only allow them to come to one a year. If that. Unless that boyfriend or girlfriend is currently in your improv group. In which case they are definitely sleeping with two of the other members.

Use this book wisely. And have a great time. I've never had more fun than onstage doing college improv. I hope you will, too.

Pictured here are the Immediate Gratification Players with their inaugural Immediate Gratification Player of the Year, Jeff Garlin.

About the Authors

Scott Levin-Gesundheit

Lead Editor, Lead Writer

Scott Levin-Gesundheit is a member of the Harvard College Class of 2011. He served as czar of the Immediate Gratification Players from 2010 to 2011. Scott got his humble comedic start at "Club Improv" at Los Altos High School. Apart from humor, his passions include tacos and politics. He currently resides in Los Altos, California.

Alasdair Wilkins

Lead Writer

Alasdair Wilkins is a member of the Harvard College Class of 2010. He has eight years of improv experience, from his high school troupe, the Baker's Dozen, to the past four years with the Immediate Gratification Players. He is currently a reporter for the science and science fiction blog io9, part of the Gawker Media network.

Ben Smith
Contributing Writer, Contributing Editor
Ben Smith is a member of the Harvard College Class of 2012. He grew up in historic Lexington, Massachusetts. Before joining the Immediate Gratification Players, Ben was a member of Lexington High School's improv troupe, the appropriately named "Improv Troupe." Besides comedy, Ben enjoys drama, romance, action, and new releases.

Kevin Burrows
Contributing Writer, Contributing Artist
Kevin is a member of the Harvard College Class of 2010. He served as czar of the Immediate Gratification Players from 2009 to 2010 and pretty much did nothing of consequence from 1988 to 2009. He currently lives in Los Angeles where his exceptional talents at weather-based small talk go sadly unused.

Brian Fithian
Contributing Writer
Brian Fithian is a member of the Harvard College Class of 2010. He served as czar of the Immediate Gratification Players from 2008 to 2009. He had no prior improv experience when he joined IGP as a freshman, but learned a tremendous amount from (and with) his fellow troupe members. He is from Poquoson, Virginia. When he is not improvising he likes fishing and relaxing with his family.

Graham Lazar
Contributing Editor
Graham Lazar is a member of the Harvard College Class of 2012. Born and raised in Chicago, Graham spent the first eighteen years of his life in the improv capital of the world. Graham's comedy heroes include all members of the Immediate Gratification Players, past and present, and his life heroes include Mike Tyson and Woody Allen.

Asher Lipson
Contributing Editor
Asher Lipson is a member of the Harvard College Class of 2012. He started improvising with the Immediate Gratification Players, but has enjoyed performing since he was a little kid. Asher is from the Berkshires in Western Massachusetts. He is currently a vegetarian and he loves to laugh.

Katherine Damm
Contributing Editor
Katherine Damm is a member of the Harvard College Class of 2013. She began improvising in high school with the William Penn Charter School's branch of ComedySportz and joined the Immediate Gratification Players as a college freshman. She lives in Philadelphia and enjoys cheese steaks and brotherly love.

Martha Farlow
Contributing Editor
Martha Farlow is a member of the Harvard College Class of 2013. She is from Needham, Massachusetts, and got her improvisational start at ImprovBoston, where she first took classes in middle school. When she is not making a fool of herself onstage, Martha enjoys long walks, word games, and doing absolutely nothing.

Christopher Frugé
Contributing Editor
Christopher Frugé is in the Harvard College Class of 2013. He joined the Immediate Gratification Players in the fall of 2009, and it was his first improv experience. Christopher enjoys reading, writing, and crazy progressive activism. He was born and raised in Houston, Texas. It was not on a ranch.

Ben Cosgrove
Contributing Writer, Contributing Artist
Ben Cosgrove is a member of the Harvard College Class of 2010. Ben is from Massachusetts and was the piano player for the Immediate Gratification Players from 2007 to 2010. He is a musician (www.bencosgrove.com) and an occasional nonfiction writer.

Jessica Napier
Contributing Artist

Jessica Napier is a member of the Harvard College Class of 2010. She grew up in London, England. As a child, she took to all sorts of performing like a duck to water, but her first experience of improvisation came with her introduction to the Immediate Gratification Players. She wishes to thank all past and present members of IGP for helping her to become the improviser that she is today.

Aneliese Palmer
Contributing Artist

Aneliese Palmer is a member of the Harvard College Class of 2012. Her career in improvisational comedy began in high school, when a friend forced her to compete in a local "Improvaganza" competition because they needed another girl. She has performed with Scared Scriptless Improv, a troupe based out of Anchorage, and she currently resides in Eagle River, Alaska. When she is not making things up, Aneliese enjoys pottery, camping, and naps.

Order Form

Meriwether Publishing Ltd.
PO Box 7710
Colorado Springs, CO 80933-7710
Phone: 800-937-5297   Fax: 719-594-9916
Website: www.meriwether.com

Please send me the following books:

_____ **So You Think You're Funny? #BK-B316 $17.95**
by The Immediate Gratification Players
A students' guide to improv comedy

_____ **Truth in Comedy   #BK-B164 $17.95**
by Charna Halpern, Del Close and Kim "Howard" Johnson
The manual of improvisation

_____ **Art by Committee (Book and DVD) $22.95**
#BK-B284
by Charna Halpern
A guide to advanced improvisation

_____ **Improv Ideas #BK-B283 $23.95**
by Justine Jones and Mary Ann Kelley
A book of games and lists

_____ **275 Acting Games: Connected #BK-B314 $19.95**
by Gavin Levy
A comprehensive workbook of theatre games for developing acting skills

_____ **The Ultimate Improv Book #BK-B248 $17.95**
by Edward J. Nevraumont, Nicholas P. Hanson and Kurt Smeaton
A complete guide to comedy improvisation

_____ **Group Improvisation #BK-B259 $16.95**
by Peter Gwinn with additional material by Charna Halpern
The manual of ensemble improv games

**These and other fine Meriwether Publishing books are available at
your local bookstore or direct from the publisher. Prices subject to
change without notice. Check our website or call for current prices.**

Name: _____ email:_____

Organization name: _____

Address: _____

City: _____ State: _____

Zip: _____ Phone: _____

❑ **Check enclosed**

❑ **Visa / MasterCard / Discover / Am. Express #** _____

Expiration
Signature: _____ *date:*   _____ / _____
       (required for credit card orders)

Colorado residents: Please add 3% sales tax.
Shipping: Include $3.95 for the first book and 75¢ for each additional book ordered.

❑ *Please send me a copy of your complete catalog of books and plays.*